PERCY JACKSON

AND THE
SWORD OF HADES

LOOK, I DIDN'T WANT TO BE A
HALF-BLOOD. I NEVER ASKED TO BE
THE SON OF A GREEK GOD.

Percy Jackson was just a normal kid, going to
school, playing basketball, skateboarding. The usual.
Until he accidentally vaporized his maths teacher.

That's when things really started going wrong.

As the son of Poseidon, God of the Sea, Percy
has faced battles with Zeus, had hand-to-claw combat
with a half-lion, half-human, and he's blown up his
school. In fact, he spends most of his time just
trying to stay alive.

The Greek gods are alive and kicking in the
twenty-first century. Get involved and seek out
the PERCY JACKSON series today.

percyjackson.co.uk

This book has been specially written and published for World Book Day 2009.

World Book Day is a worldwide celebration of books and reading, and was marked in more than thirty countries around the globe last year.

For further information please see
www.worldbookday.com

World Book Day in the UK and Ireland is made possible by generous sponsorship from National Book Tokens, participating publishers, authors and booksellers. Booksellers who accept the £1 World Book Day Token kindly agree to bear the full cost of redeeming it.

RICK RIORDAN

PERCY JACKSON

AND THE
SWORD OF HADES

PUFFIN

PUFFIN BOOKS

Published by the Penguin Group
Penguin Books Ltd, 80 Strand, London WC2R ORL, England
Penguin Group (USA) Inc., 375 Hudson Street, New York, New York 10014, USA
Penguin Group (Canada), 90 Eglinton Avenue East, Suite 700, Toronto, Ontario, Canada M4P 2Y3
(a division of Pearson Penguin Canada Inc.)
Penguin Ireland, 25 St Stephen's Green, Dublin 2, Ireland (a division of Penguin Books Ltd)
Penguin Group (Australia), 250 Camberwell Road, Camberwell, Victoria 3124, Australia
(a division of Pearson Australia Group Pty Ltd)
Penguin Books India Pvt Ltd, 11 Community Centre, Panchsheel Park, New Delhi – 110 017, India
Penguin Group (NZ), 67 Apollo Drive, Rosedale, North Shore 0632, New Zealand
(a division of Pearson New Zealand Ltd)
Penguin Books (South Africa) (Pty) Ltd, 24 Sturdee Avenue, Rosebank, Johannesburg 2196, South Africa

Penguin Books Ltd, Registered Offices: 80 Strand, London WC2R ORL, England

puffinbooks.com

First published 2009
1

Text copyright © Rick Riordan, 2009
All rights reserved

The moral right of the author has been asserted

Set in 13/21.5pt Centaur MT
Made and printed in England by Clays Ltd, St Ives plc

British Library Cataloguing in Publication Data
A CIP catalogue record for this book is available from the British Library

ISBN: 978-0-955-94468-0

www.greenpenguin.co.uk

Penguin Books is committed to a sustainable future for
our business, our readers and our planet.
The book in your hands is made from paper
certified by the Forest Stewardship Council.

Christmas in the Underworld was NOT my idea.

If I'd known what was coming, I would've called in sick. I could've avoided an army of demons, a fight with a Titan and a trick that almost got my friends and me cast into eternal darkness.

But no. I had to take my stupid English exam. So there I was the last day of the winter semester at Goode High School, sitting in the auditorium with all the other freshmen and trying to finish my I-didn't-read-it-but-I'm-pretending-like-I-did essay on *A Tale of Two Cities*, when Mrs O'Leary burst onto the stage, barking like crazy.

Mrs O'Leary is my pet hellhound. She's a shaggy black monster the size of a Hummer with razor fangs, steel-sharp claws and glowing red eyes. She's really sweet, but usually she stays at Camp Half-Blood, our demigod training camp. I was a little surprised to see her on stage, trampling over the Christmas trees and Santa's elves and the rest of the Winter Wonderland set.

Everyone looked up. I was sure the other kids were going to panic and run for the exits, but they just started snickering and laughing. A couple of the girls said, 'Awww, cute!'

Our English teacher, Dr Boring (I'm not kidding; that's his real name), adjusted his glasses and frowned.

'All right,' he said. 'Whose poodle?'

I sighed in relief. Thank gods for the Mist – the magical veil that keeps humans from seeing things the way they really are. I'd seen it bend ̶ plenty of times before, but Mrs O'Leary ̶ poodle? That was impressive.

'Um, my poodle, sir,' I spoke up. 'Sorry! It must've followed me.'

Somebody behind me started whistling 'Mary Had a Little Lamb'. More kids cracked up.

'Enough!' Dr Boring snapped. 'Percy Jackson, this is a final exam. I cannot have poodles –'

'WOOF!' Mrs O'Leary's bark shook the auditorium. She wagged her tail, knocking over a few more elves. Then she crouched on her front paws and stared at me like she wanted me to follow.

'I'll get her out of here, Dr Boring,' I promised. 'I'm finished anyway.'

I closed my test booklet and ran towards the stage. Mrs O'Leary bounded for the exit and I followed, the other kids still laughing and calling out behind me, 'See ya, Poodle Boy!'

Mrs O'Leary ran down East 81st Street towards the river.

'Slow down!' I yelled. 'Where are you going?'

I got some strange looks from pedestrians, but this was New York City, so a boy chasing a poodle probably wasn't the weirdest thing they'd ever seen.

Mrs O'Leary kept well ahead of me. She turned to bark every once in a while as if to say *Move it, slowcoach!* She ran three blocks north, straight into Carl Schurz Park. By the time I caught up with her, she leaped an iron fence and disappeared into a huge topiary wall of snow-covered bushes.

'Aw, come on,' I complained. I hadn't had a chance to grab my coat back at school. I was already freezing, but I climbed the fence and plunged into the frozen shrubbery.

On the other side was a clearing – a half acre of icy grass ringed with bare trees. Mrs O'Leary was sniffing around, wagging her tail like crazy. I didn't see anything out of the ordinary. In front of me the steel-coloured East River flowed sluggishly. White plumes billowed from the rooftops in Brooklyn. Behind me, the Upper East Side loomed cold and silent.

I wasn't sure why, but the back of my neck started to tingle. I took out my ballpoint pen and uncapped it. Immediately it grew into my bronze sword, Riptide, its blade glowing faintly in the winter light.

Mrs O'Leary lifted her head. Her nostrils quivered.

'What is it, girl?' I whispered.

The bushes rustled and a golden deer burst through. When I say golden – I don't mean yellow. This thing had metallic fur and horns that looked like genuine fourteen carat. It shimmered with an aura of golden light, making it almost too bright to look at. It was probably the most beautiful thing I'd ever seen.

Mrs O'Leary licked her lips as if she were thinking, *Deer burgers!* Then the bushes rustled again and a figure in a hooded parka leaped into the clearing, an arrow notched in her bow.

I raised my sword. The girl aimed at me – then froze.

'Percy?' She pushed back the silvery hood of her parka. Her black hair was longer than I remembered, but I knew those bright blue eyes and the silver tiara that marked her as the First Lieutenant of Artemis.

'Thalia!' I said. 'What are you doing here?'

'Following the golden deer,' she said, like that should be obvious. 'It's the sacred animal of Artemis. I figured it was some sort of sign. And, um . . .' She nodded nervously at Mrs O'Leary. 'You want to tell me what *that's* doing here?'

'That's my pet – Mrs O'Leary, no!'

Mrs O'Leary was sniffing the deer and basically not respecting its personal space. The deer butted the hellhound in the nose. Pretty soon, the two of them were playing a strange game of keep-away around the clearing.

'Percy . . .' Thalia frowned. 'This can't be a coincidence. You and me, ending up in the same place at the same time?'

She was right. Demigods didn't have coincidences. Thalia was a good friend, but I hadn't seen her in over a year, and now, suddenly, here we were.

'Some god is messing with us,' I guessed.

'Probably.'

'Good to see you, though.'

She gave me a grudging smile. 'Yeah. We get out of this in one piece, I'll buy you a cheeseburger. How's Annabeth?'

Before I could answer, a cloud passed over the sun. The golden deer shimmered and disappeared, leaving Mrs O'Leary barking at a pile of leaves.

I readied my sword. Thalia drew her bow.

Instinctively we stood back to back. A patch of darkness passed over the clearing and a boy tumbled out of it like he'd been tossed, landing in the grass at our feet.

'Ow,' he muttered. He brushed off his aviator's jacket. He was about twelve years old, with dark hair, jeans, a black T-shirt and a silver skull ring on his right hand. A sword hung at his side.

'*Nico?*' I said.

Thalia's eyes widened. 'Bianca's little brother?'

Nico scowled. I doubt he liked being announced as Bianca's little brother. His sister, a Hunter of Artemis, had died a couple of years ago, and it was still a sore subject for him.

'Why'd you bring me here?' he grumbled. 'One minute I'm in a New Orleans graveyard. The next minute — is this New York? What in Hades' name am I doing in New York?'

'We didn't bring you here,' I promised. 'We

were –' A shiver went down my back. 'We were brought together. All three of us.'

'What are you talking about?' Nico demanded.

'The children of the Big Three,' I said. 'Zeus, Poseidon, Hades.'

Thalia took a sharp breath. 'The prophecy. You don't think Kronos . . .'

She didn't finish the thought. We all knew about the big prophecy: a war was coming between the Titans and the gods, and the next child of the three major gods who turned sixteen would make a decision that saved or destroyed the world. That meant one of us. Over the last few years, the Titan lord Kronos had tried to manipulate each of us separately. Now . . . could he be plotting something by bringing us all together?

The ground rumbled. Nico drew his own sword – a black blade of Stygian iron. Mrs O'Leary leaped backwards and barked in alarm.

Too late, I realized she was trying to warn me.

The ground opened up under Thalia, Nico and me, and we fell into darkness.

I expected to keep falling forever, or maybe be squashed into a demigod pancake when we hit the bottom. But the next thing I knew, Thalia, Nico and I were standing in a garden, all three of us still screaming in terror, which made me feel pretty silly.

'What – where are we?' Thalia asked.

The garden was dark. Rows of silver flowers glowed faintly, reflecting off huge gemstones that lined the planting beds – diamonds, sapphires and rubies the size of footballs. Trees arched over us, their branches covered with orange blooms and sweet-smelling fruit. The air was cool and damp – but not like a New York winter. More like a cave.

'I've been here before,' I said.

Nico plucked a pomegranate off a tree. 'My stepmother Persephone's garden.' He made a sour face and dropped the fruit. 'Don't eat anything.'

He didn't need to tell me twice. One taste of Underworld food, and we'd never be able to leave.

'Heads up,' Thalia warned.

I turned and found her aiming her bow at a tall woman in a white dress.

At first I thought the woman was a ghost. Her dress billowed around her like smoke. Her long, dark hair floated and curled as if it were weight-less. Her face was beautiful but deathly pale.

Then I realized her dress wasn't white. It was made of all sorts of changing colours – red, blue and yellow flowers blooming in the fabric – but it was strangely faded. Her eyes were the same way, multicoloured but washed out, like the Underworld had sapped her life force. I had a feeling that in the world above she would be beautiful, even brilliant.

'I am Persephone,' she said, her voice thin and papery. 'Welcome, demigods.'

Nico squashed a pomegranate under his boot. '*Welcome?* After last time, you've got the nerve to welcome me?'

I shifted uneasily, because talking that way to a god can get you blasted into dust bunnies. 'Um, Nico —'

'It's all right,' Persephone said coldly. 'We had a little family spat.'

'*Family spat?*' Nico cried. 'You turned me into a dandelion!'

Persephone ignored her stepson. 'As I was saying, demigods, I welcome you to my garden.'

Thalia lowered her bow. 'You sent the golden deer?'

'And the shadow that collected Nico,' the goddess admitted. 'And the hellhound.'

'You controlled Mrs O'Leary?' I asked.

Persephone shrugged. 'She is a creature of the Underworld, Percy Jackson. I merely planted a suggestion in her mind that it would be fun to lead you to the park. It was necessary to bring you three together.'

'Why?' I asked.

Persephone regarded me, and I felt like cold little flowers were blooming in my stomach.

'Lord Hades has a problem,' she said. 'And if you know what's good for you, you will help him.'

We sat on a dark veranda overlooking the garden. Persephone's handmaidens brought food and drink, which none of us touched. The handmaidens would've been pretty except for the fact that they were dead. They wore yellow dresses, with daisy and hemlock wreaths on their heads. Their eyes were hollow and they spoke in the chittering bat-like voices of shades.

Persephone sat on a silver throne and studied us. 'If this were spring, I would be able to greet you properly in the world above. Alas, in winter this is the best I can do.'

She sounded bitter. After all these millennia, I guess she still resented living with Hades half the year. She looked so bleached and out-of-place, like an old photograph of springtime.

She turned towards me as if reading my thoughts. 'Hades is my husband and master, young one. I would do anything for him. But in this case I need your help, and quickly. It concerns Lord Hades' sword.'

Nico frowned. 'My father doesn't have a sword. He uses a staff in battle, and his helm of terror.'

'He *didn't* have a sword,' Persephone corrected.

Thalia sat up. 'He's forging a new symbol of power? Without Zeus's permission?'

The goddess of springtime pointed. Above the

table, an image flickered to life: skeletal weapon-smiths working over a forge of black flames, using hammers fashioned like metal skulls to beat a length of iron into a blade.

'War with the Titans is almost upon us,' Persephone said. 'My lord Hades must be ready.'

'But Zeus and Poseidon would never allow Hades to forge a new weapon!' Thalia protested. 'It would unbalance their power-sharing agreement.'

Persephone shook her head. 'You mean it would make Hades their equal? Believe me, daughter of Zeus, the Lord of the Dead has no designs against his brothers. He knew they would never under-stand, however, which is why he forged the blade in secret.'

The image over the table shimmered. A zombie weapon-smith raised the blade, still glowing hot. Something strange was set in the base — not a gem. More like . . .

'Is that a key?' I asked.

Nico made a gagging sound. 'The keys of Hades?'

'Wait,' Thalia said. 'What are the keys of Hades?'

Nico's face looked even paler than his stepmother's. 'Hades has a set of golden keys that can lock or unlock death. At least . . . that's the legend.'

'It is true,' Persephone said.

'How do you lock and unlock death?' I asked.

'The keys have the power to imprison a soul in the Underworld,' Persephone said, 'or to release it.'

Nico swallowed. 'If one of those keys has been set in the sword –'

'The wielder can raise the dead,' Persephone said, 'or slay any living thing and send its soul to the Underworld with a mere touch of the blade.'

We were all silent. The shadowy fountain gurgled in the corner. Handmaidens floated around us, offering trays of fruit and candy that would keep us in the Underworld forever.

'That's a wicked sword,' I said at last.

'It would make Hades unstoppable,' Thalia agreed.

'So you see,' Persephone said, 'why you must help get it back.'

I stared at her. 'Did you say *get it back*?'

Persephone's eyes were beautiful and deadly serious, like poison blooms. 'The blade was stolen when it was almost finished. I do not know how, but I suspect a demigod, some servant of Kronos. If the blade falls into the Titan lord's hands –'

Thalia shot to her feet. 'You allowed the blade to be stolen! How stupid was that? Kronos probably has it by now!'

Thalia's arrows sprouted into long-stemmed

roses. Her bow melted into a honeysuckle vine dotted with white and gold flowers.

'Take care, huntress,' Persephone warned. 'Your father may be Zeus, and you may be the lieutenant of Artemis, but you do *not* speak to me with disrespect in my own palace.'

Thalia ground her teeth. 'Give . . . me . . . back . . . my . . . bow.'

Persephone waved her hand. The bow and arrows changed back to normal. 'Now sit and listen. The sword could not have left the Underworld yet. Lord Hades used his remaining keys to shut down the realm. Nothing gets in or out until he finds the sword, and he is using all his power to locate the thief.'

Thalia sat down reluctantly. 'Then what do you need us for?'

'The search for the blade cannot be common knowledge,' said the goddess. 'We have locked the realm, but we have not announced why, and

Hades' servants cannot be used for the search. They must not know the blade exists until it is finished. Certainly they can't know it is missing.'

'If they thought Hades was in trouble, they might desert him,' Nico guessed. 'And join the Titans.'

Persephone didn't answer, but if a goddess could look nervous, she did. 'The thief must be a demigod. No immortal can steal another immortal's weapon directly. Even Kronos must abide by that Ancient Law. He has a champion down here somewhere. And to catch a demigod . . . we shall use three.'

'Why us?' I said.

'You are the children of the three major gods,' Persephone said. 'Who could withstand your combined power? Besides, when you restore the sword to Hades, you will send a message to Olympus. Zeus and Poseidon will not protest against Hades' new weapon if it is given to him by their own children. It will show that you trust Hades.'

'But I *don't* trust him,' Thalia said.

'Ditto,' I said. 'Why should we do anything for Hades, much less give him a super-weapon? Right, Nico?'

Nico stared at the table. His fingers tapped on his black Stygian blade.

'Right, Nico?' I prompted.

It took him a second to focus on me. 'I have to do this, Percy. He's my father.'

'Oh, no way,' Thalia protested. 'You can't believe this is a good idea!'

'Would you rather have the sword in Kronos's hands?'

He had a point there.

'Time is wasting,' Persephone said. 'The thief may have accomplices in the Underworld, and he will be looking for a way out.'

I frowned. 'I thought you said the realm was locked.'

'No prison is airtight, not even the Underworld. Souls are always finding new ways out faster than Hades can close them. You must retrieve the sword before it leaves our realm, or all is lost.'

'Even if we wanted to,' Thalia said, 'how would we find this thief?'

A potted plant appeared on the table: a sickly yellow carnation with a few green leaves. The flower listed sideways, like it was trying to find the sun.

'This will guide you,' the goddess said.

'A magic carnation?' I asked.

'The flower always faces the thief. As your prey gets closer to escaping, the petals will fall off.'

Right on cue, a yellow petal turned grey and fluttered to the ground.

'If all the petals fall off,' Persephone said, 'the flower dies. This means the thief has reached an exit and you have failed.'

I glanced at Thalia. She didn't seem too enthusiastic about the whole track-a-thief-with-a-flower thing. Then I looked at Nico. Unfortunately, I recognized the expression on his face. I knew what it was like wanting to make your dad proud, even if your dad was hard to love. In this case, *really* hard to love.

Nico was going to do this, with or without us. And I couldn't let him go alone.

'One condition,' I told Persephone. 'Hades will have to swear on the River Styx that he will never use this sword against the gods.'

The goddess shrugged. 'I am not Lord Hades, but I am confident he would do this – as payment for your help.'

Another petal fell off the carnation.

I turned to Thalia. 'I'll hold the flower while you beat up the thief?'

She sighed. 'Fine. Let's go catch this jerk.'

✳

The Underworld didn't get into the Christmas spirit. As we made our way down the palace road into the Fields of Asphodel, it looked pretty much like it had on my previous visit – seriously depressing. Yellow grass and stunted black poplar trees rolled on forever. Shades drifted aimlessly across the hills, coming from nowhere and going nowhere, chattering to each other and trying to remember who they were in life. High above us, the cavern ceiling glistened darkly.

I carried the carnation, which made me feel pretty stupid. Nico led the way since his blade could clear a path through any crowd of undead. Thalia mostly grumbled that she should've known better than to go on a quest with a couple of *boys.*

'Did Persephone seem kind of uptight?' I asked.

Nico waded through a mob of ghosts, driving

them back with Stygian iron. 'She always acts that way when I'm around. She hates me.'

'Then why did she include you in the quest?'

'Probably my dad's idea.' He sounded like he wanted that to be true, but I wasn't so sure.

It seemed strange to me that Hades hadn't given us the quest himself. If this sword was so important to him, why had he let Persephone explain things? Usually Hades liked to threaten demigods in person.

Nico forged ahead. No matter how crowded the fields were – and if you've ever seen Times Square on New Year's Eve, you'll have a pretty good idea – the spirits parted before him.

'He's handy with zombie crowds,' Thalia admitted. 'Think I'll take him along next time I go to the shopping mall.'

She gripped her bow tight, like she was afraid it would turn into a honeysuckle vine again. She didn't look any older than she had last year, and

[24]

it suddenly occurred to me she would never age again now that she was a huntress. That meant I was older than her. Weird.

'So,' I said, 'how's immortality treating you?'

She rolled her eyes. 'It's not total immortality, Percy. You know that. We can still die in combat. It's just . . . we don't ever age or get sick, so we live forever, assuming we don't get sliced to pieces by monsters.'

'Always a danger.'

'Always.' She looked around, and I realized she was scanning the faces of the dead.

'If you're looking for Bianca,' I said quietly, so Nico wouldn't hear me, 'she'd be in Elysium. She died a hero's death.'

'I know that,' Thalia snapped. Then she caught herself. 'It's not that, Percy. I was just . . . never mind.'

A cold feeling washed over me. I remembered that Thalia's mother had died in a car crash a few years ago. They'd never been close, but Thalia had never got to say goodbye. If her mother's shade was wandering around down here — no wonder Thalia looked jumpy.

'I'm sorry,' I said. 'I wasn't thinking.'

Our eyes met, and I got the feeling she understood. Her expression softened. 'It's okay. Let's just get this over with.'

Another petal fell off the carnation as we marched on.

I wasn't happy when the flower pointed us towards the Fields of Punishment. I was hoping we'd veer into Elysium so we could hang out with the beautiful people and party, but no. The flower seemed to like the harshest, evillest part of the Underworld. We jumped over a lava stream and picked our way past scenes of horrible torture. I won't describe them because you'd completely lose your appetite, but I wished I had cotton wool in my ears to shut out the screaming and the 1980s music.

The carnation tilted its face towards a hill on our left.

'Up there,' I said.

Thalia and Nico stopped. They were covered with soot from trudging through Punishment. I probably didn't look much better.

A loud grinding noise came from the other side of the hill, like somebody was dragging a washing machine. Then the hill shook with a *BOOM! BOOM! BOOM!* and a man yelled curses.

Thalia looked at Nico. 'Is that who I think it is?'

'Afraid so,' Nico said. 'The number-one expert on cheating death.'

Before I could ask what he meant, he led us to the top of the hill.

✳

The dude on the other side was not pretty, and he was not happy. He looked like one of those troll dolls with orange skin, a pot belly, scrawny legs and arms, and a big loin-cloth/diaper thing round his waist. His ratty hair stuck up like a torch. He was hopping about, cursing and kicking a boulder that was twice as big as he was.

'I won't!' he screamed. 'No, no, no!' Then he launched into a string of swear words in several different languages. If I'd had one of those jars where you put a quarter in for each bad word, I would've made around five hundred dollars.

He started to walk away from the boulder, but after three metres he lurched backwards like some invisible force had pulled him. He staggered back to the boulder and started banging his head against it.

'All right!' he screamed. 'All right, curse you!'

He rubbed his head and muttered some more

swear words. 'But this is the *last* time. Do you hear me?'

Nico looked at us. 'Come on. While he's between attempts.'

We scrambled down the hill.

'Sisyphus!' Nico called.

The troll guy looked up in surprise. Then he scrambled behind his rock. 'Oh, no! You're not fooling me with those disguises! I know you're the Furies!'

'We're not the Furies,' I said. 'We just want to talk.'

'Go away!' he shrieked. 'Flowers won't make it better. It's too late to apologize!'

'Look,' Thalia said, 'we just want —'

'La-la-la!' he yelled. 'I'm not listening!'

We played tag with him round the boulder until finally Thalia, who was the quickest, caught the old man by his hair.

'Stop it!' he wailed. 'I have rocks to move. Rocks to move!'

'I'll move your rock!' Thalia offered. 'Just shut up and talk to my friends.'

Sisyphus stopped fighting. 'You'll – you'll move my rock?'

'It's better than looking at you.' Thalia glanced at me. 'Be quick about it.' Then she shoved Sisyphus towards us.

She put her shoulder against the rock and started pushing it very slowly uphill.

Sisyphus scowled at me distrustfully. He pinched my nose.

'Ow!' I said.

'So you're really not a Fury,' he said in amazement. 'What's the flower for?'

'We're looking for someone,' I said. 'The flower is helping us find him.'

'Persephone!' He spat in the dust. 'That's one of her tracking devices, isn't it?' He leaned forward, and I caught an unpleasant whiff of old-guy-who's-been-rolling-a-rock-for-eternity.

'I fooled her once, you know. I fooled them all.'

I looked at Nico. 'Translation?'

'Sisyphus cheated death,' Nico explained. 'First he chained up Thanatos, the reaper of souls, so no one could die. Then when Thanatos got free and was about to kill him, Sisyphus told his wife not to do the correct funeral rites so he couldn't rest in peace. Sisy here – May I call you Sisy?'

'No!'

'Sisy tricked Persephone into letting him go back to the world to haunt his wife. And he didn't come back.'

The old man cackled. 'I stayed alive another thirty years before they finally tracked me down!'

Thalia was halfway up the hill now. She gritted her teeth, pushing the boulder with her back. Her expression said, *Hurry up!*

'So that was your punishment,' I said to

Sisyphus. 'Rolling a boulder up a hill forever. Was it worth it?'

'A temporary setback!' Sisyphus cried. 'I'll bust out of here soon, and when I do they'll all be sorry!'

'How would you get out of the Underworld?' Nico asked. 'It's locked down, you know.'

Sisyphus grinned wickedly. 'That's what the other one asked.'

My stomach tightened. 'Someone else asked your advice?'

'An angry young man,' Sisyphus recalled. 'Not very polite. Held a sword to my throat. Didn't offer to roll my boulder at all.'

'What did you tell him?' Nico said. 'Who was he?'

Sisyphus massaged his shoulders. He glanced up at Thalia, who was almost at the top of the hill. Her face was bright red and drenched in sweat.

'Oh . . . it's hard to say,' Sisyphus said. 'Never seen him before. He carried a long package all wrapped up in black cloth. Skis, maybe? A shovel? Maybe if you wait here, I could go look for him . . .'

'What did you tell him?' I demanded.

'Can't remember.'

Nico drew his sword. The Stygian iron was so cold it steamed in the hot, dry air of Punishment. 'Try harder.'

The old man winced. 'What kind of person carries a sword like that?'

'A son of Hades,' Nico said. 'Now *answer* me!'

The colour drained from Sisyphus's face. 'I told him to talk to Melinoe! She always has a way out!'

Nico lowered his sword. I could tell the name *Melinoe* bothered him. 'All right. What did this demigod look like?'

'Um . . . he had a nose,' Sisyphus said. 'A mouth. And one eye and –'

'One eye?' I interrupted. 'Did he have an eye patch?'

'Oh . . . maybe,' Sisyphus said. 'He had hair on his head. And –' He gasped and looked over my shoulder. 'There he is!'

We fell for it.

As soon as we turned, Sisyphus took off. 'I'm free! I'm free! I'm – ACK!' Three metres from the hill, he hit the end of his invisible leash and fell on his back. Nico and I grabbed his arms and hauled him back up to the top.

'Curse you!' He let loose with the bad words in Ancient Greek, Latin, English, French and several other languages I didn't recognize. 'I'll never help you! Go to Hades!'

'Already there,' Nico muttered.

'Incoming!' Thalia shouted.

I looked up and might have used a few swear

words myself. The boulder was bouncing straight towards us. Nico jumped one way. I jumped the other. Sisyphus yelled, 'NOOOOOOO!' as the thing ploughed into him. Somehow he braced himself and stopped it before it could run him over. I guess he'd had a lot of practice.

'Take it again!' he wailed. 'Please. I can't hold it.'

'Not again,' Thalia gasped. 'You're on your own.'

He treated us to a lot more colourful language. It was clear he wasn't going to help us any further, so we left him to his punishment.

'Melinoe's cave is this way,' Nico said.

'If this thief guy really has one eye,' I said, 'that could be Ethan Nakamura, son of Nemesis. He's the one who freed Kronos.'

'I remember,' Nico said darkly. 'But if we're dealing with Melinoe, we've got bigger problems. Come on.'

As we walked away, Sisyphus was yelling, 'All right, but this is the last time. Do you hear me? The last time!'

Thalia shuddered.

'You okay?' I asked her.

'I guess . . .' She hesitated. 'Percy, the scary thing is, when I got to the top, I thought I had it. I thought, *This isn't so hard. I can get the rock to stay.* And as it rolled down I was almost tempted to try it again. I figured I could get it the second time.'

She looked back wistfully.

'Come on,' I told her. 'The sooner we're out of here the better.'

We walked for what seemed like eternity. Three more petals withered from the carnation, which meant it was now officially half dead. The flower pointed towards a range of jagged grey hills that looked like teeth, so we trudged in that direction over a plain of volcanic rock.

'Nice day for a stroll,' Thalia muttered. 'The Hunters are probably feasting in some forest glade right about now.'

I wondered what my family was doing. My mom and stepdad, Paul, would be worried when I didn't come home from school, but it wasn't the first time this had happened. They'd figure out pretty quickly that I was on some quest. My mom would be pacing back and forth in the living room wondering if I were going to make it back to unwrap my presents.

'So who is this Melinoe?' I asked, trying to take my mind off home.

'Long story,' Nico said. 'Long, very scary story.'

I was about to ask what he meant when Thalia dropped to a crouch. 'Weapons!'

I drew Riptide. I'm sure I looked terrifying with a potted carnation in the other hand, so I put it down. Nico drew his sword.

We stood back to back. Thalia notched an arrow.

'What is it?' I whispered.

She seemed to be listening. Then her eyes widened. A ring of a dozen daemons materialized around us.

They were part humanoid female, part bat. Their faces were pug-nosed and furry, with fangs and bulging eyes. Matted grey fur and piecemeal armour covered their bodies. They had shrivelled arms with claws for hands, leathery wings that sprouted from their backs, and stubby bowed legs. They would've looked funny except for the murderous glow in their eyes.

'Keres,' Nico said.

'What?' I asked.

'Battlefield spirits. They feed on violent death.'

'Oh, wonderful,' Thalia said.

'Get back!' Nico ordered the daemons. 'The son of Hades commands you!'

The Keres hissed. Their mouths foamed. They glanced apprehensively at our weapons, but I got the feeling the Keres weren't impressed by Nico's command.

'Soon Hades will be defeated,' one of them snarled. 'Our new master shall give us free rein!'

Nico blinked. 'New master?'

The lead daemon lunged. Nico was so surprised, it might have slashed him to bits, but Thalia shot an arrow point-blank into its ugly bat face and the creature disintegrated.

The rest of them charged. Thalia dropped her bow and drew her knives. I ducked as Nico's sword whistled over my head, cutting a daemon in half. I sliced and jabbed and three or four Keres exploded around me, but more just kept coming.

'Iapetus shall crush you!' one shouted.

'Who?' I asked. Then I ran her through with

my sword. Note to self: if you vaporize monsters, they can't answer your questions.

Nico was also cutting an arc through the Keres. His black sword absorbed their essence like a vacuum cleaner, and the more he destroyed the colder the air became around him. Thalia's knives flashed and more Keres disintegrated.

'Die in pain, mortal!' Before I could raise my sword in defence, another daemon's claws raked my shoulder. If I'd been wearing armour, no problem, but I was still in my school uniform. The thing's talons sliced my shirt open and tore into my skin. My whole left side seemed to explode in pain.

Nico kicked the monster away and stabbed it. All I could do was collapse and curl into a ball, trying to endure the horrible burning.

The sound of battle died. Thalia and Nico rushed to my side.

'Hold still, Percy,' Thalia said. 'You'll be fine.'

But the quiver in her voice told me the wound was bad. Nico touched it and I yelled in pain.

'Nectar,' he said. 'I'm pouring nectar on it.'

He uncorked a bottle of the godly drink and trickled it across my shoulder. This was dangerous – just a sip of the stuff is all most demigods can stand – but immediately the pain eased. Together, Nico and Thalia dressed the wound and I only passed out a few times.

I couldn't judge how much time went by, but the next thing I remember I was propped up with my back against a rock. My shoulder was bandaged. Thalia was feeding me tiny squares of chocolate-flavoured ambrosia.

'The Keres?' I muttered.

'Gone for now,' she said. 'You had me worried for a second, Percy, but I think you'll make it.'

Nico crouched next to us. He was holding the potted carnation. Only five petals still clung to the flower.

'The Keres will be back,' he warned. He looked at my shoulder with concern. 'That wound . . . the Keres are spirits of disease and pestilence as well as violence. We can slow down the infection, but eventually you'll need serious healing. I mean a *god's* power. Otherwise . . .'

He didn't finish the thought.

'I'll be fine.' I tried to sit up and immediately felt nauseous.

'Slow,' Thalia said. 'You need rest before you can move.'

'There's no time.' I looked at the carnation. 'One of the daemons mentioned Iapetus. Am I remembering right? That's a Titan?'

Thalia nodded uneasily. 'The brother of Kronos, father of Atlas. He was known as the Titan of the West. His name means the Piercer because that's what he likes to do to his enemies. He was cast into Tartarus along with his brothers. He's supposed to be still down there.'

'But if the sword of Hades can unlock death?' I asked.

'Then maybe,' Nico said, 'it can also summon the damned out of Tartarus. We can't let them try.'

'We still don't know who *them* is,' Thalia said.

'The half-blood working for Kronos,' I said. 'Probably Ethan Nakamura. And he's starting to recruit some of Hades' minions to his side – like the Keres. The daemons think that if Kronos wins the war, they'll get more chaos and evil out of the deal.'

'They're probably right,' Nico said. 'My father tries to keep a balance. He reins in the more violent spirits. If Kronos appoints one of his brothers to be the lord of the Underworld –'

'Like this Iapetus dude,' I said.

'– then the Underworld will get a lot worse,' Nico said. 'The Keres would like that. So would Melinoe.'

'You still haven't told us who Melinoe is.'

Nico chewed his lip. 'She's the goddess of ghosts – one of my father's servants. She oversees the restless dead that walk the earth. Every night she rises from the Underworld to terrify mortals.'

'She has her own path into the upper world?'

Nico nodded. 'I doubt it would be blocked. Normally, no one would even think about trespassing in her cave. But if this demigod thief is brave enough to make a deal with her –'

'He could get back to the world,' Thalia supplied. 'And take the sword to Kronos.'

'Who would use it to raise his brothers from Tartarus,' I guessed. 'And we'd be in big trouble.'

I struggled to my feet. A wave of nausea almost made me black out, but Thalia grabbed me.

'Percy,' she said, 'you're in no condition –'

'I have to be.' I watched as another petal withered and fell off the carnation. Four left before doomsday. 'Give me the potted plant. We have to find the cave of Melinoe.'

As we walked, I tried to think about positive things: my favourite basketball players, my last conversation with Annabeth, what my mom would make for Christmas dinner – anything but the pain. Still, it felt like a sabre-toothed tiger was chewing on my shoulder. I wasn't going to be much good in a fight, and I cursed myself for letting down my guard. I should never have got hurt. Now Thalia and Nico would have to haul my useless butt through the rest of the mission.

I was so busy feeling sorry for myself I didn't notice the sound of roaring water until Nico said, 'Uh-oh.'

About fifteen metres ahead of us, a dark river churned through a gorge of volcanic rock. I'd seen the Styx, and this didn't look like the same river. It was narrow and fast. The water was black as ink. Even the foam churned black. The far bank was only ten metres across, but that was too far to jump, and there was no bridge.

'The River Lethe.' Nico cursed in Ancient Greek. 'We'll never make it across.'

The flower was pointing to the other side – towards a gloomy mountain and a path leading up to a cave. Beyond the mountain, the walls of the Underworld loomed like a dark granite sky. I hadn't considered that the Underworld might have an outer rim, but this appeared to be it.

'There's got to be a way across,' I said.

Thalia knelt next to the bank.

'Careful!' Nico said. 'This is the River of Forgetfulness. If one drop of that water gets on you, you'll start to forget who you are.'

Thalia backed up. 'I know this place. Luke told me about it once. Souls come here if they choose to be reborn, so they totally forget their former lives.'

Nico nodded. 'Swim in that water, and your mind will be wiped clean. You'll be like a newborn baby.'

Thalia studied the opposite bank. 'I could shoot an arrow across, maybe anchor a line to one of those rocks.'

'You want to trust your weight to a line that isn't tied off?' Nico asked.

Thalia frowned. 'You're right. Works in the movies, but . . . no. Could you summon some dead people to help us?'

'I could, but they would only appear on my side of the river. Running water acts as a barrier against the dead. They can't cross it.'

I winced. 'What kind of stupid rule is that?'

'Hey, I didn't make it up.' He studied my face. 'You look terrible, Percy. You should sit down.'

'I can't. You need me for this.'

'For what?' Thalia asked. 'You can barely stand.'

'It's water, isn't it? I'll have to control it. Maybe I can redirect the flow long enough to get us across.'

'In your condition?' Nico said. 'No way. I'd feel safer with the arrow idea.'

I staggered to the edge of the river.

I didn't know if I could do this. I was the child of Poseidon, so controlling salt water was no problem. Regular rivers . . . maybe, if the river spirits were feeling cooperative. Magical Underworld rivers? I had no idea.

'Stand back,' I said.

I concentrated on the current – the raging black water rushing past. I imagined it was part of my own body, that I could control the flow, make it respond to my will.

I wasn't sure, but I thought the water churned and bubbled more violently, as if it could sense my presence. I knew I couldn't stop the river altogether. The current would back up and flood the whole valley, exploding all over us as soon as I let it go. But there was another solution.

'Here goes nothing,' I muttered.

I raised my arms like I was lifting something over my head. My bad shoulder burned like lava, but I tried to ignore it.

The river rose. It surged out of its banks, flowing up and then down again in a great arc – a raging black rainbow of water six metres high. The riverbed in front of us turned to drying mud, a tunnel under the river just wide enough for two people to walk side by side.

Thalia and Nico stared at me in amazement.

'Go,' I said. 'I can't hold this for long.'

Yellow spots danced in front of my eyes. My wounded shoulder nearly screamed in pain. Thalia and Nico scrambled into the riverbed and made their way across the sticky mud.

Not a single drop. I couldn't let a single drop of water touch them.

The River Lethe fought me. It didn't want to be forced out of its banks. It wanted to crash down on my friends, wipe their minds clean and drown them. But I held the arc.

Thalia climbed the opposite bank and turned to help Nico.

'Come on, Percy!' she said. 'Walk!'

My knees were shaking. My arms trembled. I took a step forward and almost fell. The water arc quivered.

'I can't make it,' I called.

'Yes, you can!' Thalia said. 'We need you!'

Somehow, I managed to climb down into the riverbed. One step, then another. The water surged above me. My boots squished in the mud.

Halfway across, I stumbled. I heard Thalia scream, 'No!' And my concentration broke.

As the River Lethe crashed down on me, I had time for one last desperate thought: *Dry.*

I heard the roar and felt the crash of tons of

water as the river fell back into its natural course. But . . .

I opened my eyes. I was surrounded by darkness, but I was completely dry. A layer of air covered me like a second skin, shielding me from the effects of the water. I struggled to my feet. Even this small effort to stay dry – something I'd done many times in normal water – was almost more than I could handle. I slogged forward through the black current, blind and doubled over with pain.

I climbed out of the River Lethe, surprising Thalia and Nico, who jumped back a good two metres. I staggered forward, collapsed in front of my friends and passed out cold.

The taste of nectar brought me around. My shoulder felt better, but I had an uncomfortable buzz in my ears. My eyes felt hot, like I had a fever.

'We can't risk any more nectar,' Thalia was saying. 'He'll burst into flames.'

'Percy,' Nico said. 'Can you hear me?'

'Flames,' I murmured. 'Got it.'

I sat up slowly. My shoulder was newly bandaged. It still hurt, but I was able to stand.

'We're close,' Nico said. 'Can you walk?'

The mountain loomed above us. A dusty trail snaked up a hundred metres or so to the mouth of a cave. The path was lined with human bones for that extra-cosy feel.

'Ready,' I said.

'I don't like this,' Thalia murmured. She cradled the carnation, which was pointing towards the cave. The flower now had two petals left, like very sad bunny ears.

'A creepy cave,' I said. 'The goddess of ghosts. What's not to like?'

As if in response, a hissing sound echoed down the mountain. White mist billowed from the cave like someone had turned on a dry-ice machine.

In the fog, an image appeared — a tall woman with dishevelled blonde hair. She wore a pink bathrobe and had a wine glass in her hand. Her face was stern and disapproving. I could see right through her, so I knew she was a spirit of some kind, but her voice sounded real enough.

'Now you come back,' she growled. 'Well, it's too late!'

I looked at Nico and whispered, 'Melinoe?'

Nico didn't answer. He stood frozen, staring at the spirit.

Thalia lowered her bow. 'Mother?' Her eyes teared up. Suddenly she looked about seven years old.

The spirit threw down her wine glass. It shattered and dissolved into fog. 'That's right, girl. Doomed to walk the earth, and it's your fault! Where were you when I died? Why did you run away when I needed you?'

'I – I –'

'Thalia,' I said. 'It's just a shade. It can't hurt you.'

'I'm more than that,' the spirit growled. 'And Thalia knows it.'

'But – *you* abandoned *me*,' Thalia said.

'You wretched girl! Ungrateful runaway!'

'Stop!' Nico stepped forward with his sword drawn, but the spirit changed form and faced him.

This ghost was harder to see. She was a woman in an old-fashioned black velvet dress with a matching hat. She wore a string of pearls and white gloves, and her dark hair was tied back.

Nico stopped in his tracks. 'No . . .'

'My son,' the ghost said. 'You were taken from me so young. I died of grief, wondering what had happened to you and your sister.'

'Mama?'

'No, it's my mother,' Thalia murmured, as if she still saw the first image.

My friends were helpless. The fog began thickening around their feet, twining around their legs like vines. The colours seemed to fade from their clothes and their faces, as if they too had become shades.

'Enough,' I said, but my voice hardly worked. Despite the pain, I lifted my sword and stepped towards the ghost. 'You're not anybody's mama!'

The ghost turned towards me. The image flickered, and I saw the goddess of ghosts in her true form.

You'd think after a while I would stop getting freaked out by the appearance of Greek ghoulies, but Melinoe caught me by surprise. Her right half was pale chalky white, like she'd been drained of blood. Her left half was pitch black and hardened like mummy skin. She wore a golden dress and a golden shawl. Her eyes were empty black voids and, when I looked into them, I felt as if I were seeing my own death.

'Where are your ghosts?' she demanded in irritation.

'My . . . I don't know. I don't have any.'

She snarled. 'Everyone has ghosts – deaths you regret. Guilt. Fear. Why can I not see yours?'

Thalia and Nico were still entranced, staring at the goddess as if she were their long-lost mother. I thought about other friends I'd seen die – Bianca di Angelo, Zoë Nightshade, Lee Fletcher, to name a few.

'I've made my peace with them,' I said. 'They've passed on. They're not ghosts. Now let my friends go!'

I slashed at Melinoe with my sword. She backed up quickly, growling in frustration. The fog dissipated around my friends. They stood blinking at the goddess as if they were now seeing how hideous she was.

'What is *that*?' Thalia said. 'Where –'

'It was a trick,' Nico said. 'She fooled us.'

'You are too late, demigods,' Melinoe said. Another petal fell off my carnation, leaving only one. 'The deal has been struck.'

'What deal?' I demanded.

Melinoe made a hissing sound, and I realized it was her way of laughing. 'So many ghosts, my young demigod. They long to be unleashed. When Kronos rules the world, I shall be free to walk among mortals both night and day, sowing terror as they deserve.'

'Where's the sword of Hades?' I demanded. 'Where's Ethan?'

'Close,' Melinoe promised. 'I will not stop you. I will not need to. Soon, Percy Jackson, you will have many ghosts. And you will remember me.'

Thalia notched an arrow and aimed it at the goddess. 'If you open a path to the world, do you really think Kronos will reward you? He'll cast you into Tartarus along with the rest of Hades' servants.'

Melinoe bared her teeth. 'Your mother was right, Thalia. You are an angry girl. Good at running away. Not much else.'

The arrow flew, but as it touched Melinoe she dissolved into fog, leaving nothing but the hiss of her laughter. Thalia's arrow hit the rocks and shattered harmlessly.

'Stupid ghost,' she muttered.

I could tell she was really shaken up. Her eyes were rimmed with red. Her hands trembled. Nico looked just as stunned, like someone had smacked him between the eyes.

'The thief . . .' he managed. 'Probably in the cave. We have to stop him before –'

Just then, the last petal fell off the carnation. The flower turned black and wilted.

'Too late,' I said.

A man's laughter echoed down the mountain.

'You're right about that,' a voice boomed. At the mouth of the cave stood two people – a boy with an eye patch and a three-metre-tall man in a tattered prison jumpsuit. The boy I recognized: Ethan Nakamura, son of Nemesis. In his hands was an unfinished sword — a double-edged blade of black Stygian iron with skeletal designs etched in silver. It had no hilt, but set in the base of the blade was a golden key, just like I'd seen in Persephone's image. The key was glowing, as if Ethan had already invoked its power.

The giant man next to him had eyes of pure silver. His face was covered with a scraggly beard and his grey hair stuck out wildly. He looked thin and haggard in his ripped prison clothes, like he'd spent the last few thousand years at the bottom of a pit, but even in this weakened state he looked plenty scary. He held out his hand and a giant spear appeared. I remembered what Thalia had said about Iapetus: *His name means the Piercer because that's what he likes to do to his enemies.*

The Titan smiled cruelly. 'Thanks to this fine sword, I have been raised from Tartarus. And now I will destroy you.'

'Master!' Ethan interrupted. He was dressed in combat fatigues with a backpack slung over his shoulder. His eye patch was crooked, his face smeared with soot and sweat. 'We have the sword. We should —'

'Yes, yes,' the Titan said impatiently. 'You've done well, Nawaka.'

'It's Nakamura, master.'

'Whatever. I'm sure my brother Kronos will reward you. But now we have killing to attend to.'

'My lord,' Ethan persisted. 'You're not at full power. We should ascend and summon your brothers from the upper world. Our orders were to flee.'

The Titan whirled on him. 'FLEE? Did you say *FLEE*?'

The ground rumbled. Ethan fell on his butt and scrambled backwards. The unfinished sword of Hades clattered to the rocks. 'M-m-master, please –'

'IAPETUS DOES NOT FLEE! I have waited three aeons to be summoned from the pit. I want revenge, and I will start by killing these weaklings!'

He levelled his spear at me and charged.

If he'd been at full strength, I have no doubt he would have pierced me right through the middle. Even weakened and just out of the pit, the guy was fast. He moved like a tornado, slashing so quickly I barely had time to dodge the strike before his spear impaled the rock where I'd been standing.

I was so dizzy I could barely hold my sword. Iapetus yanked the spear out of the ground, but as he turned to face me Thalia shot his flank full of arrows from his shoulder to his knee. He roared and turned on her, looking more angry than hurt. Ethan Nakamura tried to draw his own sword, but Nico yelled, 'I don't think so!'

The ground erupted in front of Ethan. Three armoured skeletons climbed out and engaged Ethan, pushing him back. The sword of Hades still lay on the rocks. If I could only get to it . . .

Iapetus slashed with his spear and Thalia leaped out of the way. She dropped her bow so she could draw her knives, but she wouldn't last long in close combat.

Nico left Ethan to the skeletons and charged Iapetus. I was already ahead of him. It felt like my shoulder was going to explode, but I launched myself at the Titan and stabbed downward with Riptide, impaling the blade in the Titan's calf.

'AHHHH!' Golden ichor gushed from the wound. He whirled and the shaft of his spear slammed into me, sending me flying.

I crashed into the rocks, right next to the River Lethe.

'YOU DIE FIRST!' Iapetus roared as he hobbled towards me. Thalia tried to get his attention by zapping him with an arc of electricity from her knives, but she might as well have been a mosquito. Nico stabbed with his sword but Iapetus knocked him aside without even looking. 'I will kill you all! Then I will cast your souls into the eternal darkness of Tartarus!'

My eyes were full of spots. I could barely move. Another inch and my head would fall into the river.

The river.

I swallowed, hoping my voice still worked. 'You're — you're even uglier than your son,' I taunted the Titan. 'I can see where Atlas gets his stupidity from.'

Iapetus snarled. He limped forward, raising his spear.

I didn't know if I had the strength, but I had to try. Iapetus brought the spear down and I lurched sideways. The shaft impaled the ground right next to me. I reached up and grabbed his shirt collar, counting on the fact that he was off-balance as well as hurt. He tried to regain his footing, but I pulled him forward with my whole body weight. He stumbled and fell, grabbing my arms in a panic, and together we pitched into the Lethe.

FLOOOOOM! I was immersed in black water.

I prayed to Poseidon that my protection would hold and, as I sank to the bottom, I realized I was still dry. I knew my own name. And I still had the Titan by the shirt collar.

The current should've ripped him out of my hands, but somehow the river was channelling itself around me, leaving us alone.

With my last bit of strength, I climbed out of

the river, dragging Iapetus with my good arm. We collapsed on the riverbank – me perfectly dry, the Titan dripping wet. His pure silver eyes were as big as moons.

Thalia and Nico stood over me in amazement. Up by the cave, Ethan Nakamura was just cutting down the last skeleton. He turned and froze when he saw his Titan ally spreadeagled on the ground.

'My – my lord?' he called.

Iapetus sat up and stared at him. Then he looked at me and smiled.

'Hello,' he said. 'Who am I?'

'You're my friend,' I blurted out. 'You're . . . Bob.'

That seemed to please him greatly. 'I am your friend Bob!'

Clearly, Ethan could tell things were not going his way. He glanced at the sword of Hades lying in the dirt, but before he could lunge for it, a silver arrow sprouted in the ground at his feet.

'Not today, kid,' Thalia warned. 'One more step and I'll pin your feet to the rocks.'

Ethan ran – straight into the cave of Melinoe. Thalia took aim at his back, but I said, 'No. Let him go.'

She frowned, but lowered her bow.

I wasn't sure why I wanted to spare Ethan. I guess we'd had enough fighting for one day, and in truth I felt sorry for the kid. He would be in enough trouble when he reported back to Kronos.

Nico picked up the sword of Hades reverently. 'We did it. We actually did it.'

'We did?' Iapetus asked. 'Did I help?'

I managed a weak smile. 'Yeah, Bob. You were great.'

We got an express ride back to the palace of Hades. Nico sent word ahead, thanks to some ghost he summoned out of the ground, and within a few minutes the Three Furies themselves arrived to ferry us back. They weren't thrilled about lugging Bob the Titan, too, but I didn't have the heart to leave him behind, especially after he noticed my shoulder wound, said, 'Owie,' and healed it with a touch.

Anyway, by the time we arrived in the throne room of Hades, I was feeling great. The Lord of the Dead sat on his throne of bones, glowering at us and stroking his black beard like he was contemplating the best way to torture us. Persephone sat next to him, not saying a word, as Nico explained about our adventure.

Before we gave back the sword, I insisted that Hades take an oath not to use it against the gods. His eyes flared like he wanted to incinerate me, but finally he made the promise through clenched teeth.

Nico laid the sword at his father's feet and bowed, waiting for a reaction.

Hades glared at his wife. 'You defied my direct orders.'

I wasn't sure what he was talking about, but Persephone didn't react, even under his piercing gaze.

Hades turned back to Nico. His gaze softened just a little, like *rock* soft rather than *steel.* 'You will speak of this to no one.'

'Yes, lord,' Nico agreed.

The god glared at me. 'And if your friends do not hold their tongues, I will cut them out.'

'You're welcome,' I said.

Hades stared at the sword. His eyes were full of anger and something else — something like hunger. He snapped his fingers. The Furies fluttered down from the top of his throne.

'Return the blade to the forges,' he told them. 'Stay with the smiths until it is finished, and then return it to me.'

The Furies swirled into the air with the weapon,

and I wondered how soon I would be regretting this day. There were ways around oaths, and I imagined Hades would be looking for one.

'You are wise, my lord,' Persephone said.

'If I were wise,' he growled, 'I would lock you in your chambers. If you ever disobey me again –'

He let the threat hang in the air. Then he snapped his fingers and vanished into darkness.

Persephone looked even paler than usual. She took a moment to smooth her dress then turned towards us. 'You have done well, demigods.' She waved her hand and three red roses appeared at our feet. 'Crush these, and they will return you to the world of the living. You have my lord's thanks.'

'I could tell,' Thalia muttered.

'Making the sword was your idea,' I realized. 'That's why Hades wasn't there when you gave us the mission. Hades didn't know the sword was missing. He didn't even know it existed.'

'Nonsense,' the goddess said.

Nico clenched his fists. 'Percy's right. You wanted Hades to make a sword. He told you no. He knew it was too dangerous. The other gods would never trust him. It would undo the balance of power.'

'Then it got stolen,' Thalia said. '*You* shut down the Underworld, not Hades. You couldn't tell him what had happened. And you needed us to get the sword back before Hades found out. You used us.'

Persephone moistened her lips. 'The important thing is that Hades has now accepted the sword. He will have it finished, and my husband will become as powerful as Zeus or Poseidon. Our realm will be protected against Kronos . . . or any others who try to threaten us.'

'And we're responsible,' I said miserably.

'You've been very helpful,' Persephone agreed. 'Perhaps a reward for your silence —'

'You'd better go,' I said, 'before I carry you down to the Lethe and throw you in. Bob will help me. Won't you, Bob?'

'Bob will help you!' Iapetus agreed cheerfully.

Persephone's eyes widened, and she disappeared in a shower of daisies.

Nico, Thalia and I said our goodbyes on a balcony overlooking Asphodel. Bob the Titan sat inside, building a toy house out of bones and laughing every time it collapsed.

'I'll watch him,' Nico said. 'He's harmless now. Maybe . . . I don't know. Maybe we can retrain him to do something good.'

'Are you sure you want to stay here?' I asked. 'Persephone will make your life miserable.'

'I have to,' he insisted. 'I have to get close to my dad. He needs a better adviser.'

I couldn't argue with that. 'Well, if you need anything –'

'I'll call,' he promised. He shook hands with Thalia and me. He turned to leave, but he looked at me one more time. 'Percy, you haven't forgotten my offer?'

A shiver went down my spine. 'I'm still thinking about it.'

Nico nodded. 'Well, whenever you're ready.'

After he was gone, Thalia said, 'What offer?'

'Something he told me last summer,' I said. 'A possible way to fight Kronos. It's dangerous. And I've had enough danger for one day.'

Thalia nodded. 'In that case, still up for dinner?'

I couldn't help but smile. 'After all that, you're hungry?'

'Hey,' she said, 'even immortals have to eat. I'm thinking cheeseburgers at McHale's.'

And, together, we crushed the roses that would return us to the world.

PERCY'S SUMMER CAMP REPORT

DEAR PERCY JACKSON,
BELOW IS YOUR PROGRESS REPORT FOR THE SUMMER, WHICH WILL BE SENT HOME TO YOUR PARENTS. WE ARE HAPPY TO REPORT THAT YOUR MARKS ARE PASSABLE, SO YOU WILL NOT BE FED TO THE HARPIES AT THE PRESENT TIME.

SINCERELY,
CHIRON, ACTIVITIES DIRECTOR
DIONYSUS, CAMP DIRECTOR

ACTIVITY	GRADE	COMMENTS
MONSTER MAIMING	A	Percy shows great aptitude at lopping off limbs.
DEFENCE	B	Percy almost got killed several times this summer. Good job!
SWORDFIGHTING	A+	Percy's swordfighting skills are excellent. However, it would be better if he could fight without dousing himself in salt water first.
ARCHERY	C-	On the bright side, he has not shot any of his fellow campers for weeks.
JAVELIN THROWING	B	Percy has been practising! His last throw almost hit the target. True, he knocked a bronze bull's head off, but that is easily fixed.
CHARIOT RACING	A	In Percy's last race, he not only won but left most of the other chariots in flames. Well done!

SIGNED: *Percy Jackson*

HORRIBLE HISTORIES

GROOVY GREEKS

DEARY/BROWN

NATIONAL
BOOK
tokens

■ SCHOLASTIC

This book has been specially written and published for World Book Day 2009.

World Book Day is a worldwide celebration of books and reading, and was marked in over 30 countries around the globe last year.

For further information please see www.worldbookday.com

World Book Day in the UK and Ireland is made possible by generous sponsorship from National Book Tokens, participating publishers, authors and booksellers. Booksellers who accept the £1 World Book Day Token kindly agree to bear the full cost of redeeming it.

Scholastic Children's Books,
Euston House, 24 Eversholt Street,
London, NW1 1DB, UK

A division of Scholastic Ltd
London ~ New York ~ Toronto ~ Sydney ~ Auckland
Mexico City ~ New Delhi ~ Hong Kong

First published in the UK by Scholastic Ltd, 1996
This abridged edition published 2009

Text copyright © Terry Deary, 1996
Illustrations © Martin Brown, 1996
All rights reserved

10 digit ISBN 0 955 94468 6
13 digit ISBN 978 0955 94468 0

Made and printed in England by Clays Ltd, St Ives plc

2 4 6 8 10 9 7 5 3 1

The right of Terry Deary and Martin Brown to be identified as the author and illustrators of this work respectively has
been asserted by them in accordance with the Copyright, Designs and Patents Act, 1988.

CONTENTS

Terry Deary was born at a very early age, so long ago he can't remember. But his mother, who was there at the time, says he was born in Sunderland, north-east England, in 1946 – so it's not true that he writes all *Horrible Histories* from memory. At school he was a horrible child only interested in playing football and giving teachers a hard time. His history lessons were so boring and so badly taught, that he learned to loathe the subject. *Horrible Histories* is his revenge.

Martin Brown was born in Melbourne, on the proper side of the world. Ever since he can remember he's been drawing. His dad used to bring back huge sheets of paper from work and Martin would fill them with doodles and little figures. Then, quite suddenly, with food and water, he grew up, moved to the UK and found work doing what he's always wanted to do: drawing doodles and little figures.

Introduction

History can be horrible. And do you know who to blame?

No, it's the Greeks!

The Greeks invented history about 2,500 years ago …

Inventing history is just one of the things we have to thank them for. They had the idea for plays, for the Olympic Games – even the camera…

Funny you should mention that. Here is a book on the groovy Greeks. A book that will tell you all the things that teacher doesn't tell you. The things you really want to know. The hilarious stories and the horror stories.

Groovy Greek timeline

BC

1600 – 1200 First Greek civilizations, ruled by the mighty Mycenaean lords of Crete.

About 1180 The siege of Troy – Troy loses to the famous wooden horse trick.

About 1100 The state of Sparta starts.

776 First recorded Olympic games.

About 750 – 550 Greeks take to the seas and become great traders.

About 730 Greeks produce the first works of written poetry in the world. Groovy Homer is the most famous.

640 World's first roof tiles manufactured at Temple of Hera at Olympia.

About 600 Thales, the Greek scientist, announces that the entire earth is actually floating in water.

585 Scientist Thales predicts an eclipse of the sun.

About 550 First plays performed. King Croesus of Lydia has gold and silver coins made; the first coins with writing on them.

7

About 530 Peisistratus of Athens creates a library.

About 520 Alcmaeon of Croton finds out about the human body by cutting up dead ones – groovy, eh?

490 Persians invade Greece – beaten by Greeks at The Battle Marathon.

486 The first comedy drama at Athens.

480 Xerxes of Persia attacks the Greeks. The battle of Thermopylae. Spartan heroes die.

460 Athens v Sparta and Persia.

431 – 404 Athens tries to get too bossy so the others fight the Peloponnesian War. Sparta becomes top dog.

430 Great Plague of Athens kills Athenian leader, Pericles, not to mention a quarter of all the Athenian people.

413 A defeat at Syracuse for the army of Athens followed by…

404 The Fall of Athens.

About 400 Greek army engineers invent the stomach bow - the first type of crossbow.

371 Spartans lose to new top dog, the Thebans.

336 Alexander the Great becomes king of Macedon when his dad is assassinated. In just ten years he conquers the old enemy, Persia.

330 Aristotle invents the 'camera obscura' – a sort of pinhole camera and the idea behind today's film and television - now that really was groovy!

323 Alexander the Great dies. His generals divide up his empire.

322 The end of democracy in Athens when the Macedons take over.

215 Archimedes invents war machines like the catapult – they keep the Romans out for three years.

213 Archimedes has mirrors set along the harbour walls – they dazzle the Romans and set fire to their boats . . . Romans delayed for a while but. . .

212 Here come the Romans.

146 Greece part of the Roman Empire.

AD

393 Romans abandon Olympic Games – they don't happen again for 1500 years.

The gruesome gods

Before the groovy Greeks came the mighty Mycenaean people, who ruled Greece. Their greatest palace was on the island of Crete – it was so posh the queen had the world's first flushing toilet. Then the palaces were wrecked and the Mycenaean way of life went too. No more flushing toilets. What went wrong? Was it. . .

• war and attack from outside
• earthquakes
• disease and plague
• drought and famine
• change of climate?

They've all been suggested by historians. But, like the disappearance of the dinosaurs, no one really knows for sure.

The *Dorian* people moved down into Greece. They forgot how to write so we don't know a lot about those days. Historians call them the *Dark* Ages.

So, without writing, the history was preserved in stories. And, as the years passed, the stories became wilder and more unlikely. Legends, in fact.

The Greeks loved horror stories best of all. One Greek writer said that Greek children should not be told stories like this one (just as grown-ups today say you should not watch certain horror films).

But this book is a Horrible History and this story has a PG rating.

Do *not* read this story if you suffer from nightmares or at least read it with your eyes closed so you don't suffer the most gory bits.

YOU HAVE BEEN WARNED!

Bringing up baby

Cronos was the chief god. You'd think that would make him happy, but no. Somebody told him that one of his children would take his place.

'Can't have that,' Cronos complained. 'Here, Mrs Cronos, pass me that baby!'

'What for?'

'Never mind daft questions. Just pass me that baby.'

Mrs Cronos passed across their new-born child. 'Here! What you doin' of with that baby?' she cried.

'Eatin' it.'

'Eatin' it! You great greedy lummock. You've just had your tea. You can't be hungry again already.'

11

'I'm not hungry,' the great god growled. 'Just there's this prophecy about one of my children taking my throne. No kid, no take-over, that's the way I look at it.'

'You don't want to go takin' no notice of them horry-scopes,' Mrs Cronos sighed.

'Don't pay to take chances is what I always say,' Cronos said smugly. 'Pass them indigestion tablets.'

Time passed, as time does, and Mrs Cronos had more baby gods… and Cronos ate every last one. Well, not the *very* last one. Mrs Cronos was getting fed up with his gruesome guzzling. 'I'll put a stop to his little game,' she smirked as she hid the new baby, Zeus, under her bed. She picked up a big rock, wrapped it in a baby blanket and dropped it in the cot.

In walked Cronos. 'Where is it?'

'In the cot.'

'Ugly little beggar, isn't he?' the head god said, squinting at the boulder.

'Takes after his father then,' Mrs Cronos mumbled.

BON APPETIT DEAR

'Crunchy as well,' her husband said, swallowing teeth.

'Probably cos he's *bolder* than the rest,' Mrs Cronos agreed.

Cronos sat down heavily on a royal couch. 'Ooooh! I think I've eaten someone who disagrees with me.' 'It's possible,' Mrs Cronos sniffed. 'A lot of people disagree with you, sweetheart.'

'Ooooh!' The god groaned and clutched his stomach. 'I think I'm going to be sick!'

'Not on the new carpet, my love. There's a bowl over there,' Mrs Cronos warned him.

Cronos gave a heavenly heave and threw up not just his stony snack, but all the other baby gods as well. 'Just goes to show,' Mrs Cronos smiled happily. 'You can't keep a good god down!'

And did the young gods grow up to overthrow their dreadful dad? What do you think?

13

Don't feel too sorry for Cronos. He'd killed his own father, Uranus, and scattered the bits into the oceans. Cronos and the old gods were driven out by Zeus and the new gods. These new gods were much more fun. They were really one big, unhappy family. Always arguing, fighting and doing nasty things to each other.

Zeus ruled the earth and the sky from his home on the top of mount Olympus. Of all the groovy gods, Zeus was the grooviest. In a competition he got the top job. When he wasn't flirting with human women he was frying somebody with a thunderbolt.

Zeus's brother, Poseidon, ruled the sea. A job for a real drip. Old Pos wasn't too happy with this because he was a bad loser. That's why he sulked and went stomping around, whipping up the seas with a fork and creating storms. What a stirrer!

HELP!

Answer:

1 Women! The Greeks thought they were sly and lying. They attracted men so that they couldn't live without them – at the same time they were such a nuisance men couldn't live with them either. Women were a great help when it came to sharing a man's wealth but no help at all when he was poor. Of course this legend is utter nonsense – if you don't believe me then ask any woman.

Quick quiz

Prometheus, a young god, liked humans so he stole fire from the gods and gave it to men on earth. But top god, Zeus, punished men by creating something new and terrible on earth. What were these terrible things?

1 women

2 flies

3 teachers

A third brother, Hades, was the real loser. He won the job of ruling the underworld. That must have been hell!

Fight like a Greek

The wooden heads of Troy

Everybody knows the story of the wooden horse of Troy. But can you believe it? Those Trojan twits saw a wooden horse standing outside the gates of the city…

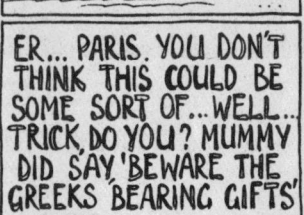

17

Everyone thinks it's a wonderful story. No one stops to ask, 'Would the Trojans really be that stupid?' But, if they *did* ask that question, the answer would have to be 'Yes.' If brains were gunpowder the Trojans wouldn't have had enough to blow their helmets off. Because they were tricked into letting the groovy Greeks into their city a *second* time.

That's right. Everyone knows about the wooden horse trick. Teachers forget to tell you about the *second* one over 800 years later in 360 BC. . .

Tricking a Trojan. . . again
Charidemus was fed up. He paced up and down in his tent and rubbed a strong hand through his greying hair. He complained, 'I'll never capture Troy. The walls are just too strong . . . and the Trojans don't look as if they're starving to death, do they?'

'No, sir,' his young lieutenant mumbled. 'Perhaps if we made a wooden horse and. . .'

Charidemus glared at him. 'Thank you. You are the fiftieth person to suggest that. The Trojans won't fall for that old trick again. Next time they'll just set fire to the wooden horse. Would you like to volunteer to sit inside it, eh? See if I'm right?'

The young man turned red and said, 'No, sir.'

He was relieved to hear someone approaching the tent. He jumped to the door.

'Password?'

'Ajax,' the man called.

The lieutenant opened the flap and said, 'Enter, friend.'

The guard stepped through, pulled on a short chain

18

and dragged a ragged man through after him. The guard stood to attention. 'Spy, sir. Caught him stealing food. Permission to execute him, sir?' he barked.

General Charidemus peered at the prisoner. The man's clothes were dusty but quite rich. 'Not yet, Captain. Leave us together.'

The guard saluted and strode out. Charidemus nodded to a cushion. 'Sit down,' he ordered. 'Your name?'

The prisoner grinned. 'Damon.' He was a wiry man with dark eyes that seemed to dart around and couldn't meet anyone else's gaze.

'And you've come out from Troy to steal our food? Are things that bad inside the city then?'

Damon smiled slyly. 'You Greeks eat better than the Trojans. Even before the siege the king gave us poor rations.'

'You don't like the king? Then why work for him?' the Greek general asked.

The prisoner shrugged. 'It's a job.'

Charidemus leaned forward. 'And if I offered you a job? A better paid and better fed job?'

Damon looked at his thumb and slowly placed it in his mouth. 'I'd be happy to work for you. I'd be loyal to you.'

The general's eyes were hard as iron as he replied, 'Oh, you'd be loyal, Damon. Men who betray me die ... but they die very slowly.'

The prisoner squirmed on his cushion and gave a nervous smile. 'What do you want me to do?'

'I want you to be my wooden horse, Damon. Listen carefully and I'll tell you exactly what I want you to do…'.

It took a week for Charidemus to prepare the plan. His young lieutenant was nervous. As he tightened the buckle on his general's armour he asked, 'How do you know Damon won't betray us?'

The general tested the weight of his short sword. 'Damon is greedy but he's not stupid. He knows that we will take Troy sooner or later. If we have to wait too long to get inside he knows we'll be angry. We'll certainly kill the Trojan men – including him. But if he helps

us he lives – and doesn't have to go to bed hungry any more.'

Charidemus slid the sword into his belt. 'Pass me my cloak.'

The young man took the large, filthy cloak and slid it over his general's wide shoulders. A hood covered the man's square head. He arranged the cloak to cover the weapons, dusted his hands and gave a nod. 'You'll pass as a poor traveller, sir.' The lieutenant changed too.

The general strode out of his tent and met a dozen men dressed the same way. No one spoke. Charidemus led the way from the torch-lit camp on to the stony road to Troy. A small man sat quietly on a horse and watched them approach.

'Is everything ready, Damon?' the general asked softly.

'It is,' the small man smiled. He turned his horse and walked slowly back towards the city gates. The Greek soldiers dragged their sandals and began to limp towards the enemy city.

'Who goes there?' a guard cried from a gate tower.

'Damon!' the traitor cried.

'Ah, so it is! What have you got with you?'

'The Greeks are growing careless. I went to their camp and found some of our captured men with just a single guard. I killed him and brought them back,' Damon lied. 'But let me in quickly. They're weak and sick!'

'Aye, Damon … oh, you'd better give the password.'

'Castor,' Damon said quickly.

The gates creaked slowly open. The man on the horse rode in – the soldiers trudged behind him.

As the gates closed the men stood in the shadow of the wall and shrugged off their cloaks. They climbed the stone stairways to the gate towers and the walls.

The Trojan defenders had no chance. They were looking for Greeks outside the walls – they didn't expect the attack to come from within.

Charidemus cut the throat of the last guard and let the limp body drop into the dark and dusty ditch that ran outside the wall. The Greeks gathered in the tower above the gate.

'Now we wait for the rest of our army…' the general began, but his lieutenant hurried to the walls and looked over. There was a rattle of stones on the road as a body

of armed men arrived and halted.

'They're here, sir, but they're too early!' the young man gasped.

'Either that or they aren't *our* men,' Charidemus said.

'How can we tell in the darkness?'

'The password, man, the password … you know, "Wooden Horse". Quick! Challenge them,' the general ordered.

'Who goes there?' the lieutenant called.

'Friend!' came the reply.

'Give the password.'

After a moment a voice called, 'Castor!'

The Greeks looked at General Charidemus. 'Let them in. If we don't they'll raise the alarm before our men get here. Hide behind the gates. As soon as the last man is in, you come out. Kill them. Kill every last one!'

The Greeks trotted down the stairs to their positions while the general and his lieutenant turned the winches that opened the gates. There was the sound of marching feet, cries of surprise and fear, the clash of weapons, then the silence of death.

From the darkest shadow of the Trojan street a small man gave a grim smile as he sat astride his horse. A horse that had led the enemy into Troy … again.

23

The savage Spartans

The first great state to grow after the Dark Ages was Sparta. The Spartan people were a bit odd. They believed they were better than anyone else. If the Spartans wanted more land then they just moved into someone else's patch. If someone was already living there the Spartans just made them slaves. In short, they were the ungrooviest lot in the whole of Greece.

Of course, a lot of people didn't enjoy being slaves. They argued with the Spartans in the only language the Spartans knew – the language of violence. They were probably the toughest of the Greek peoples because they were always having to fight to prove how good they were.

But it wasn't enough to train young men to fight. The training started from the day you were born.

Ten foul facts

1 Children were trained for fitness with running, wrestling, throwing quoits and javelins – and that was just the girls!

2 Girls also had to strip for processions, dances and temple services. That way they wouldn't learn to show off with fine clothes.

3 The marriage custom of Sparta was for a young man to pretend to carry his bride off by violence. The bride then cut off her hair and dressed like a man. The bridegroom rejoined the army and had to sneak off to visit his new wife.

4 A new-born baby was taken to be examined by the oldest Spartans. If it looked fit and strong they said, 'Let it live.' If it looked a bit sickly it was taken up a mountain and left to die.

5 A child didn't belong to its parents – it belonged to the State of Sparta. At the age of seven a child was sent off to join a 'herd' of children. The toughest child was allowed to become leader and order the others about. The old men who watched over them often set the children fighting amongst each other to see who was the toughest.

6 At the age of 12 they were allowed a cloak but no tunic. They were only allowed a bath a few times a year.

THAT THASOS IS A CLEANLINESS FREAK

YEAH...THAT'S HIS THIRD BATH THIS YEAR

7 Children slept on rushes that they gathered from the river bank themselves. If they were cold in winter then they mixed a few thistles in with the reeds … the prickling gave them a feeling of warmth.

8 The Spartan children were kept hungry. They were then encouraged to steal food – sneakiness is a good skill if you're out on a battlefield. If they were caught stealing they'd be beaten. They weren't beaten for stealing, you understand – they were beaten for being careless enough to get caught. Sometimes the young men were beaten just to toughen them up. If the beating killed the youth then it was just bad luck.

YOU SHOULD BE A LOT TOUGHER NOW... DEAD, BUT TOUGHER

9 Older boys had younger boys to serve them. If the younger boy did something wrong then a common punishment was a bite on the back of the hand.

10 If you cried out while you were fighting then not only were you punished but your best friend was punished as well.

Of course, the savage Spartans were no worse than some of their enemies, such as the Scythians. The historian, Herodotus (485 - 425 BC), described the horrors of the Scythians...

In a war, it is the custom of a Scythian soldier to drink the blood of the first man he kills. The heads of all enemies killed in battle are taken to the king; a head represents a token which, allows the soldier a share in the loot – no head no loot. He strips the skin off the head by

making a circular cut round the ears and shaking out the skull; then he scrapes the flesh off the skin with an ox's rib, and when it is clean works it supple with his fingers. He hangs these trophies on the bridle of his horse like handkerchiefs and is very proud of them. The finest warrior is the one who has the most scalps. Many Scythians sew scalps together to make cloaks and wear them like the cloak of a peasant.

The boy who didn't cry 'fox'

One Spartan story shows you how peculiar the Spartans really were. It's a story about a good little Spartan boy.

How to be a good Spartan 1: Pinch whatever you like – but don't get caught

He stole a fox cub belonging to somebody else.

How to be a good Spartan 2: Don't give up without a struggle

The boy was seen running away from the scene of the theft and arrested. But before they caught him he just had time to stuff the fox cub up his tunic.

How to be a good Spartan 3: Cheat, lie and trick your way out of trouble

The boy's master asked the boy where the fox cub was. The boy replied, 'Fox cub? What fox cub? I don't know anything about a fox cub!'

How to be a good Spartan 4: It's better to be a dead hero than a live whinger

The master's questioning went on … and on. Until suddenly the boy fell down. Dead. When the guards examined the body they found the fox cub had eaten its way into the boy's guts. The tough Spartan lad hadn't given any sign that he was suffering and he hadn't given in, even though it cost him his life.

Could you be as boldly deceitful as the Spartan boy?

Thermopylae

The story of the boy and the fox might not be true – it simply shows the sort of people the Spartans admired. But the story of the battle of Thermopylae is a1most certainly true. Again it shows the Spartans dying rather than giving in.

There were just 300 Spartans led by King Leonidas defending the narrow pass of Thermopylae against tens of thousands of Persians. The Persian leader, Xerxes, sent spies to report how many soldiers were defending the pass. He couldn't believe the Spartans would be daft enough to fight and die. Xerxes didn't know the Spartans.

But the Spartans were not just unafraid. They were really cool about it. They spent the time before the battle oiling their bodies and combing their hair – now that was groovy.

How to be a good Spartan 5: When you're in trouble, think of something witty to say

The Spartans were warned that the Persians had so many archers that their arrows would blot out the sun. Dioneces, the Spartan general, said, 'That's good. We'll have a bit of shade to fight the battle.'

How to be a good Spartan 6: Stay cooler than an iced lolly

The Spartans held on for a week. Then a traitor guided the Persians to a secret pathway that led them behind the Spartans. The 300 Spartans were massacred. As they fought to the death some lost their swords. They battled on with their fists and their teeth.

Could you stay as cool as a Spartan in danger?

Did you know… ?

One horrible historical way of proving you were a good Spartan was to be whipped at the altar of the god, Artemis. The one who suffered the most lashes was the toughest. Bleeding half to death – sometimes *all the way* to death – but *tough*. Ah yes, a *perfect* Spartan.

The spooky Spartan

Pausanius was a great Spartan general who helped to defeat the Persians in 479 BC. But the Spartans thought he was getting too big-headed and they asked him to return to Sparta to explain – or be punished.

Pausanius was not amused. He wrote to the Persian king, Xerxes, and offered to betray Sparta. Off went the messenger to Xerxes. But that messenger wondered why other messengers before him hadn't come back. So he opened the letter and read it. There on the end was a little message for Xerxes…

blah blah blah
blah blah, blah
blah…

lots of love
Pausanius

P.S. Kill the
messenger so he
can't talk.

The messenger took the letter to the Spartans instead of to Xerxes – wouldn't you? The Spartans sent a force to kill Pausanius. The general fled to the temple of Athena where he sheltered in a small building. 'You can't lay a finger on me here. I'm on sacred ground,' he said.

'Right,' the leader of the assassins said. 'We won't lay a finger on you.' And they didn't. They just bricked up the door and left him to starve to death. That should have been the end of Pausanius. The trouble was his ghost started wandering round the temple making such hideous noises that the priestess was losing customers. In the end she sent for a magician – a sort of groovy Greek Ghostbuster – to get rid of him … finally.

The odd Athenians

Deadly Draco
The people of Athens were very different from the Spartans. One of their first rulers was a man called Draco. The Athenians thought the Spartans were pretty brutal, but the laws of Draco were nearly as cruel. He wrote the first law book for Athens, and criminals were executed for almost any crime. Under Draco's laws…

• you could have someone made your personal slave if they owed you money
• the theft of an apple or a cabbage was punishable by death
• people found guilty of idleness would be executed.

Draco said…

Yes it's unfair. Little crimes and big crimes get the same punishment. If only I could think of a punishment worse than death for the serious ones.

Seven hundred years later a Greek writer, Plutarch, said …

Draco's laws were not written in ink but in blood.

Other Greeks thought that Draco's laws were better than no laws. (The people who thought this were not the ones who Draco had executed, of course.)

Playful Peisistratus

Another ruler, Peisistratus, wasn't quite so harsh. He was still a 'tyrant' – in Greece that was someone who took control of the state by force - but he stayed there only as long as the people agreed with what he was doing.

Peisistratus made the people pay heavy taxes – ten per cent of all they earned – but at least he had a sense of humour.

One day he visited a farrner. The farrner didn't recognize Peisistratus.

'WHAT DO YOU GET OUT OF THIS LAND?'

'NOTHING BUT ACHES AND PAINS, I WISH PEISISTRATUS WOULD TAKE HIS TEN PER CENT OF THOSE'

Peisistratus laughed – and ordered that the old farmer need never pay taxes again.

Plotting Peisistratus

Peisistratus became very unpopular and the people of Athens were turning against him. Then one day he drove his cart into the market place in a terrible state. He and his mules were cut and bleeding. 'I've been attacked by assassins!' he cried. 'I barely escaped with my life.'

HOW COME HE GETS ALL THE ATTENTION?

The Athenians were worried they would lose their leader – not a popular leader, but the only leader they had. They organized the strongest and most brutal Athenian men to be his bodyguards. He then used them to seize control of the city.

The attack on Peisistratus had put him in power. Just as he meant it to. For there had been *no* attack. The crafty leader had simply made the wounds himself!

Who killed the ox?

The Athenians weren't as ruthless as the Spartans. But they had their own funny little ways. One of the strangest customs of Athens involved the sacrifice of an ox in the temple. Killing the ox wasn't strange in itself. It's what the Athenians did *afterwards* that was curious. They held a trial to decide, 'Who killed the ox?'

I BLAME THE GIRLS WHO CARRIED THE WATER THAT SHARPENED THE AXE!

WE BLAME THE MAN WHO SHARPENED THE AXE AND THE KNIFE

I BLAME THE MAN WHO TOOK THE KNIFE AND THE AXE

I BLAME THE MAN WHO HIT THE OX WITH THE AXE

I BLAME THE MAN WHO STABBED THE OX WITH THE KNIFE

I BLAME THE KNIFE

WHAT HAVE YOU GOT TO SAY FOR YOURSELF, KNIFE?

IN THAT CASE I FIND THE KNIFE GUILTY OF THE OX'S MURDER. I SENTENCE THE KNIFE TO DEATH BY DROWNING. THROW THE KNIFE IN THE SEA

TO BE BLUNT I CAN'T SEA THE POINT

Horrible hemlock

The Athenians didn't just have strange ways of killing knives. They also killed each other in unusual ways.

After they had lost the war with Sparta, the Athenians looked for someone to blame. They blamed the old teacher, Socrates. Being a rather groovy guy, he was always hanging around with young people, telling them not to believe in the old gods. (That's a bit like your own teacher telling you not to believe in Father Christmas.) In Athens this was punishable by death.

But the Athenians didn't kill the old teacher – they told him to kill himself with poison! Plato described the gruesome scene ...

The man who was to give the poison came in with it ready mixed in a cup. Socrates saw him and said, 'Good Sir, you understand these things. What do I have to do?'

Just drink it and walk around until your legs begin to feel heavy, then lie down. It works very quickly.'

The man gave Socrates the cup.

The teacher took it cheerfully, without trembling, and without even turning pale. He just looked at the man and said, 'May I drink a toast?'

'You may,' the man replied.

'Then I drink to the gods and pray that we will be just as happy after death as we were in life.'

Then he drank the poison quickly and cheerfully. Until then most of us had held back our tears. But when we saw him drinking, the tears came in floods. I covered my face and wept – not for him but for myself; I had lost such a good friend.

Socrates looked at us and said sternly, 'I have heard that a person should be allowed to die in silence. So control yourselves and be quiet.' We stopped crying.

The teacher lay down. The man with the poison squeezed his foot. Socrates said he felt nothing. He said that when the poison reached the heart he would be gone.

As the numbness reached his waist Socrates called to young Crito. He said, 'Crito, we owe Asclepius a sacrifice. Be sure you pay him. Don't forget.'

[Asclepius was the god of healing.]

'Of course,' Crito replied. 'Is there anything else you want?'

But Socrates didn't reply.

This was the end of our friend.

The best, wisest and most honest person I have ever known.

What a hero! Probably the only teacher in history to die so nobly. Would your teacher be as brave?

Unfortunately you'll never have the chance to find out ... Boots the Chemist does not sell hemlock.

Dreadful democracy

Most countries today are run as *democracies* – that is to say every adult has a vote on which laws are passed and how the government spends its money.

Athens, being really groovy, had the first democracy. But because they still had a lot to learn, they didn't quite get it right…

Alexander the Great-er

Many parts of Greece competed for overall power, including a small kingdom in the north of Greece called Macedon. Some historians have even said that Macedon wasn't Greek at all.

First came Philip, king of Macedon. He defeated the Athenians and then told them he wanted them to attack the old enemy … Persia.

Then there was a small hitch in Philip's plan … he died. But that was only a tiny complication for the plan. (A rather bigger complication for Philip, of course.) Philip's son was greater and even groovier than him. Alexander the Great-er in fact…

Alexander - This is Your Life

YOU WERE BORN ALEXANDER, IN 356 BC: THE GREATEST GREEK EVER

DON'T CALL ME A GREEK, SUNSHINE. THE THE GREEKS CALLED MY DAD A BARBARIAN

YET YOU ADMIRED THE GREEK HEROES. YOU LOVED HOMER'S POETRY SO MUCH YOU CARRIED HIS STORY OF TROY EVERYWHERE, YOUR OLD TEACHER ARISTOTLE TOLD US

HE SLEPT WITH IT UNDER HIS PILLOW ACTUALLY

AND YOU HAD YOUR CHANCE WHEN YOU WERE JUST TWENTY YEARS OLD. YOUR FATHER, KING PHILIP DIED. TONIGHT WE PROUDLY PRESENT HIS GHOST...
DIED. I WAS MURDERED. STABBED BY MY OWN BODYGUARD. AND I THINK I KNOW WHO PUT HIM UP TO IT, ALEXANDER. IT WAS Y...
I DENY IT!
YOU SET OFF TO CONQUER THE WORLD. YOU DEFEATED THE PERSIANS THEN MARCHED ON TO EGYPT AND THEN THROUGH ASIA
BUT YOU COULDN'T BEAT YOUR OWN SOLDIERS COULD YOU ALEX?
THAT'S RIGHT. YOU REACHED INDIA AND YOUR SOLDIERS REFUSED TO GO ANY FURTHER. WHAT DID THE GREAT ALEXANDER DO?
HE SULKED. WENT INTO HIS TENT FOR THREE DAYS AND SULKED
YOU KEPT POWER BY HAVING PEOPLE EXECUTED IF THEY OPPOSED YOU. EVEN YOUR FRIEND PARMENIO
REMEMBER WHEN YOU GAVE ME THE CHOP, ALEX MY OLD MATE?
YOU GOT DRUNK AND STABBED ANOTHER FRIEND
IT'S TOUGH AT THE TOP

The knotty problem

Alexander entered Gordium and was told that the wagon of King Gordius was tied to its shafts with a knot that no one could untie. A legend said that the man who finally untied it would rule all Asia. How did Alexander unfasten the wagon from its shafts?

Answer: He took out his sword and cut through the knot.

Live like a Greek

Polybius' Checkerboard

The Greeks were very groovy with numbers. Polybius, born in 200 BC, was a Greek historian of Rome. He was one of 1,000 hostages taken to Rome in 168 BC. His main history books contained 40 volumes, but he also had time to invent this code, now known as Polybius' Checkerboard.

Each letter has a pair of numbers – the horizontal (across) number followed by the vertical (up-down). So, 'B' is 1-2, but F is 2-1. The word 'Yes' is 54 15 43. Get it?

	1	2	3	4	5
1	A	B	C	D	E
2	F	G	H	I/J	K
3	L	M	N	O	P
4	Q	R	S	T	U
5	V	W	X	Y	Z

Then work out this…

44 23 15 22 42 15 15 25 44 15 11 13 23 15 42 11 33
11 53 24 32 11 33 14 15 42 12 42 34 45 22 23 44 44
23 15 21 24 42 43 44 43 45 33 – 14 24 11 31 44 34
22 42 I5 I5 13 15.

Did you know… ?

Polybius' Checkerboard may have been a good way of sending secret messages. But a Greek called Histiaeus found a better one!

He was imprisoned by the Persians but was allowed to send a letter to his cousin Aristagoras. The Persians studied the message carefully. They could see no code or secret meaning. The message was a perfectly harmless letter. They let a slave take the letter to Aristagoras.

As soon as the slave arrived he said to Aristagoras, 'Shave my head.' Aristagoras shaved the slave's head. Tattooed on his scalp was the real message. 'Lead a rebellion against the Persians.' Cool, eh?

Make a pinhole camera

The Greeks also invented other groovy devices which are still important to us today. One of the cleverest was the camera obscura – or the 'pinhole' camera. A Greek artist covered a window with a dark material, then punched a small hole through. An upside-down image of the scene was seen on the inside wall and traced by the artist.

You could have a go at making your own, slightly smaller version:

1 Make a box of black card, 20 x 10 x 10 cm.
2 Make a small pinhole in black paper at one end.
3 Place grease-proof paper across the other end.
4 Hold it up to a bright scene.
5 The scene will be 'projected' on to the grease-proof paper.

Note: this image will be upside-down - you may have to stand on your head to get the best view!

Making a dodgy drachma

The Greeks had banks. There are no records of bank robbers ... but there were people who tried to cheat the banks out of lots of money. Here's how to do it. . .

1 Go to the bank and say, 'I want 10,000 drachmas to buy a ship. I'll fill it with corn and sell it on the other side of the Mediterranean. When the ship returns with the money for the corn I'll pay back the loan.'

2 The bank agrees. The Greek banks even agree that if the ship sinks (and you lose all their money) then you don't have to pay them a thing.

3 You buy a cheap ship and put a little bit of cheap corn in it. You spend about 5,000 drachmas and keep the other 5,000 drachmas for yourself.

4 Just as the ship reaches deep water you saw through the keel at the bottom of the boat. This will make it sink.

5 When the boat begins to sink you jump in the lifeboat, paddle back home and say to the bank, 'Sorry, you've lost your 10,000 drachmas!' and have a good laugh because you've earned yourself a quick 5,000 just for getting your feet wet.

Good idea, eh? And it nearly worked for the villainous ship owner, Hegestratos, and his partner, Zenothemis. But it all went wrong at stage 4.

Zenothemis kept the passengers chatting on the deck one night while Hegestratos crept down to saw through the bottom of the ship.

45

One of the passengers heard the noise and went down to investigate. Hegestratos was caught and had to escape. He fled along the deck and jumped into the waiting lifeboat. Or rather he *tried* to jump into the lifeboat. It was dark. He missed the little boat, fell in the sea ... and drowned. Served him right.

The ship reached the shore safely and the bank got Zenothemis to pay back the money. So Hegestratos ended up dead ... not rich.

Let the punishment fit the crime

Alexandria was a city in Egypt but ruled by the Greeks. Around 250 BC they had a set of laws which might give some idea of how the Greek law worked.

Can you match the crime to the punishment? Just remember the law wasn't completely fair. Especially if you were a slave.

Crime	Punishment
1 A free man strikes another free man or free woman.	**a)** A hundred lashes
2 A slave strikes a free man or free woman.	**b)** Fine of 100 drachmas
3 A drunk person injures somebody else.	**c)** A hundred lashes
4 A free man threatens another with wood, iron or bronze.	**d)** Fine of 100 drachmas
5 A slave threatens another with wood, iron or bronze.	**e)** Fine of 200 drachmas

If a master didn't want his slave to receive the 100 lashes then he had to pay 200 drachma, or 2 drachma a blow.

If you argued with a fine then you could go to court. But be careful. If you lost then you had to pay double for crime 1 or treble for crime 4.

Woe for women

Being a slave in ancient Greece wasn't much fun. Being a woman wasn't too groovy either. The Spartan women lived like men – the Athenian women lived like slaves. They were told what to do and what not to do – and they didn't have anything like the freedom that the free men enjoyed...

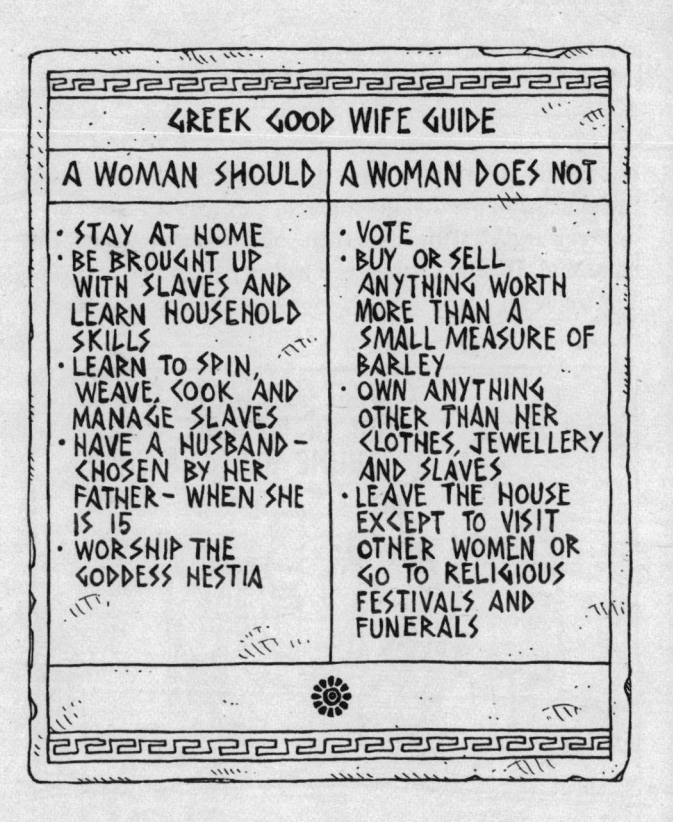

GREEK GOOD WIFE GUIDE

A WOMAN SHOULD	A WOMAN DOES NOT
• STAY AT HOME • BE BROUGHT UP WITH SLAVES AND LEARN HOUSEHOLD SKILLS • LEARN TO SPIN, WEAVE, COOK AND MANAGE SLAVES • HAVE A HUSBAND – CHOSEN BY HER FATHER – WHEN SHE IS 15 • WORSHIP THE GODDESS HESTIA	• VOTE • BUY OR SELL ANYTHING WORTH MORE THAN A SMALL MEASURE OF BARLEY • OWN ANYTHING OTHER THAN HER CLOTHES, JEWELLERY AND SLAVES • LEAVE THE HOUSE EXCEPT TO VISIT OTHER WOMEN OR GO TO RELIGIOUS FESTIVALS AND FUNERALS

Groovy girls

The women of Attica, the region surrounding Athens, were different from the women living in Athens. They helped their husbands in the fields. They also had a curious way of preparing their daughters for marriage.

Girls aged about 13 were sent to the Brauron temple of the goddess, Artemis. There they prepared to be mature young women, and good wives, by doing what?

1 Learning how to fire bows and arrows, to throw spears, to mend armour and sharpen swords.
2 Praying to the goddess for wisdom, and learning the secret spells to keep husbands happy and healthy.
3 Running and dancing through the woods with no clothes on pretending to be she-bears.

Answer: 3 The idea was they got their wildness 'out of their systems' before they settled down to marriage. The Brauron temple proved very popular with Greek girls around 370–380 BC.

However, girls, you should not try this at your **local place of worship** – you'd only get arrested, or photographed by the boys in your class, or catch pneumonia ... or all three.

I'M BEGINNING TO REALLY ENJOY GREEK HISTORY

Dress like a Greek

Instead of running naked through the local woods, you could find out what it was like to be a groovy Greek by dressing like one. Here's a simple groovy costume to make.

(**Warning**: Only suitable for summer weather.)

1 Fold an oblong cloth as shown – do *not* use Mum's best sheets for this – use Dad's.

2 Fold it again.

3 Wrap it round the body and pin it at each shoulder – the Greeks didn't have safety pins, but you can cheat and use a couple.

4 Fasten the open side with pins. Tie a belt around the waist. See picture 4 … here's one I made earlier.

5 You are now ready to be seen in public. Try running around and find out why they took them off for sports and games.

This sort of clothing is known as a *Doric Chiton*. Women's were the same design but it went down to the ankle.

Test your teacher

Teachers don't know everything – they just try to kid you that they do. Test their true brain power with these questions on the groovy Greeks...

1 Aristotle the great Greek teacher had a favourite meat. What was it?

a) camel

b) turkey

c) horse liver

2 The great playwright, Aeschylus, is supposed to have died when an eagle flew over his head and dropped something on it. What did the eagle drop?

a) a tortoise

b) a hare

c) a stone

A HARE ON THE HEAD

3 As well as the Olympic games there were games in Isthmia. The winners at the Isthmian games were given a crown as a prize. What was the crown made of?

a) celery
b) rhubarb
c) gold

4 Before clever Aristotle came along, the Greeks had a strange belief about elephants. What was it?

a) an elephant has no knee joints so it goes to sleep leaning against a tree
b) elephants never forget
c) eating elephant meat makes you strong

5 Which team sport did the Ancient Greeks enioy that we still play today?

a) hockey
b) soccer
c) volleyball

6 The Greek teacher, gorgeous Gorgias, said that 'nothing exists' … not even himself. He nearly didn't. He had a peculiar birth. Where was he born?

a) in his dead mother's coffin
b) on a mountain in a snow storm
c) on board a sinking ship

7 The Spartan youths tried out their military training by doing what for their town?

a) becoming secret police and murdering troublemakers
b) mending roads and keeping the streets clean
c) becoming servants in old people's homes and cooking for them

8 How far did the Greek explorer, Pytheas, sail?

a) Britain and the North Sea

b) Crete in the Mediterranean

c) America and the Atlantic

9 The Greeks invented a new weapon in the 4th century BC. They set fire to inflammable liquids then threw them over enemy ships or enemy cities. What is this weapon called?

a) Greek fire

b) Zeus's revenge

c) flaming dangerous

10 A sacred plant was sprinkled on graves. But we don't consider it sacred today. What is it?

a) parsley

b) cabbage

c) garlic

Test yourself

Now test yourself. See how many answers you can remember by arranging the following into the right order...

A	B	C
The playwright, Aeschylus,	invented a new weapon called	hockey
A sacred plant	sailed to	a camel
Aristotle, the great Greek teacher,	died when hit on the head by	an elephant going to sleep leaning against a tree
A Greek sportsman	was born in	a tortoise
A Greek sailor	was sprinkled on grave and called	the secret police
A Spartan youth	enjoyed the team sport called	celery
The Greek explorer, Pytheas,	won a crown made from	Greek fire
The Greek teacher, Gorgias,	believed in	the North Sea
A winner at the Isthmian games	trained in	parsley
An early Greek person	enjoyed meat from	his dead mother's coffin

Awesome Olympics

The groovy Greeks liked nothing better than a contest. The first Olympic contests were simple foot races. The first few Olympics had just one race on one day – a race of about 190 metres or the length of the stadium.

A second race – twice the length – was added in the 14th Olympics, and a still longer race was added to the 15th competition, four years later. But new events were added until the meeting lasted five days. There was even a Junior Olympics for kids.

• The bad news, girls … females were banned from the ancient Olympics.

• The bad news, boys … clothes were banned for the male athletes.

Choose your champion

You may wish to try an Olympic contest against the class next door. First you need to have a contest in your own class and choose your champion to represent you. Then go and cheer your champion as they compete against rival class champions.

Here's what to do. First choose your judges. They must train as judges (or referees) for ten months before the Olympics. They must also be honest. (You could have a problem finding an honest adult.) Agree the starting time and place and let the competitors battle it out.

• foot race – 200 metres

• double foot race – 400 metres

• standing long jump – with a kilo weight held in each hand to swing you through the air

• quoit-throwing (nearest to a fixed spot wins)
• javelin

After the contest...

1 Give the winners crowns made from the branches of a wild olive tree that grows in a sacred grove. (If you can't find one then make cardboard crowns from a sacred cornflakes packet.)

2 Call out the victor's name and country to the assembled crowds. (Or just phone the local newspaper.)

3 When the victor returns to their home they enter through a special gap knocked in the city wall. (Might be better if you *didn't* knock down the school wall. That's there for a purpose – to stop wild pupils escaping.)

4 The victor is treated with special favours – they either pay no taxes, or have free meals at the president's house for life. (Perhaps you could offer your victor a lifetime of free school dinners.)

5 Don't forget to cheer the loser. Losers have feelings too. (An Olympic wrestler called Timanthes lost his strength as he grew older. He was so upset he lit a big fire – then threw himself into it.)

Some groovy Olympic games you might not like to try

Mule-racing – smelly.
Relay – a bit hot. The god, Prometheus, stole fire from the gods and brought it down to earth for humans. But the humans had to escape from the other avenging gods. They ran with torches. The Olympic relay was run with flaming torches instead of batons, in memory of Prometheus. If the torch goes out your team loses. And if you grab the wrong end of the torch from the last runner ... ouch!

IT'S NOT MY HAND I'M WORRIED ABOUT!

Four-horse chariot race – dangerous. The poet Homer described an accident...

> *Eumelos was thrown out of the chariot beside the wheel. The skin was ripped from the elbows, nose and mouth, and his forehead smashed in over the eyebrows. His eyes filled with tears and his powerful voice was silenced.*

A bit rougher than your school rounders match, eh?

Hoplite racing – heavy, but not groovy. Wearing full armour and carrying weapons, this was hard work – try running with a couple of dustbins strapped to your back and that's how it might feel.

HOPLITE, NOT LIGHT HOP!

Trumpeters' competition – deafening.

Pancration … what? Pancration was a bit of a mixture of boxing and wrestling. The only rule was that there were no rules, apart from no biting and no gouging out the eyes. Just flatten the opponent. You could…
• strangle
• kick
• arm-twist
• jump up and down on your opponent.
Quite good if you're a winner. Painful for a loser.

Boxing – ordinary old boxing? Yes, harmless little fisticuffs – unless you do it the ancient Greek way, as the horrible historical story of Creugas and Damoxenos shows…

The Greek Guardian
still only 20 obols
Creugas the Corpse Claims Crown

In the Olympic heavyweight championship yesterday Damoxenos, the Dark Destroyer, beat challenger Creugas… and lost the title!

In a sensational contest the two men were both defending their unbeaten records. A crowd of two thousand sat on the grass in the afternoon sunshine to enjoy a fight to the end. They didn't know what an end it was going to be.

Boos

Big Damoxenos was booed as he stepped on to the grass and had leather wrapped around his mighty fists. The handsome Creugas was cheered as he stepped forward. The voice of the referee rang out across the grassy circle.

'Remember, slaps with the open hand, punches with the fist or blows with the back of the hand are allowed. Kicking is permitted, but no head butting. Understand?'

'Yes sir,' Creugas answered boldly. Big Damoxenos just grunted.

'The fight goes on without a break until one man has had enough,' the little ref went on. 'Show you are beaten by raising your right hand in the air. Understand?'

Damoxenos just sneered. 'I'll not need to remember that,' he boasted. 'I'll not be surrendering.'

Hammer

The crowd booed again as the referee stepped back. 'Box!' he cried and Damoxenos lunged forward. He swung his fist like a mighty hammer at Creugas's head but the young man jumped back and flicked a fist at the champion's head.

That was the pattern of the fight. Big Damoxenos lumbering round, swinging huge punches but unable to catch the slippery Creugas. Just as the crowd was growing restless, the sun sank down and the referee called a halt.

'We cannot have a draw,' he cried. 'The contest will be decided by a single blow struck by each man.'

First

The crowd seemed to like that and they closed in to get a better view.

'You go first, wimp,' Damoxenos growled. The big man held his arms by his sides – the crowd held its breath.

Creugas struck a hammer blow to the champion's head. The big man just laughed. 'My turn.'

'The young man shook his head and waited for the blow that would surely knock him senseless. It didn't.

Instead the big ox hit Creugas cruelly under the ribs with straight fingers. His sharp finger nails tore through the young man's skin. He pulled back his hand and jabbed again. This time he tore out the challenger's guts.

The crowd gasped as Creugas fell lifeless to the ground.

Cheat

The ref ran forward. 'One blow is all that is allowed. You took *two* blows, Damoxenos, you cheat. I hereby disqualify you. I declare that Creugas is the champion!'

The crowd cheered with joy. The new champ was not available for comment.

His manager said, 'The boy done well. Deserved that win. We'll have a few drinks later to celebrate.'

Creugas will always be remembered as a champion who had guts.

Did you know…? Olympically speaking

1 There was a fine for cheating. The cheat had to pay for an expensive statue of the god Zeus. And at Olympus there were an awful lot of Zeus statues before the Greek Olympics ended. There must have been a lot of cheats.

2 The main form of cheating was to have a really good set of horses in the chariot race then have a bet that you would *lose* the race. You made sure you lost the race by pretending to whip the horses to go faster … while secretly tugging at the reins to slow them up. This 'pulling' of horses to win money still goes on today.

3 The Greek Olympics were banned by the rotten Romans. The Romans didn't much like sport when they conquered the Greeks. The Romans preferred their own groovy 'games'… like fights to the death between gladiators … and they built huge coliseums to stage the contests. But they let the beaten Greeks keep their Olympics until miserable Roman Emperor, Theodosius, abolished them in 394 AD.

4 The Greek Olympics had competitions in music, public speaking and theatre as well.

5 The Olympics vanished for 1500 years. They were revived in 1896 by Pierre de Coubertin, a young French nobleman, and since then they have been staged every fourth year. The ancient Greek Olympics were held in honour of Zeus, and all wars would cease during the contests. The Olympics came first. Sadly, in the modern Olympics, war came first; the games stopped during World War I and World War II (1916, 1940, 1944).

6 A cook, Coroibus of Elis, was the first recorded winner.

7 The boy athlete, Pisidorus, took his mum to the Olympics. Because women were banned, she had to be disguised as his trainer.

8 ... and, talking about trainers. There are quite a few 'Nikes' at modern Olympics. But did you know that Nike was the goddess of victory, who watched over all athletic contests?

9 A sports arena was one 'stadion' (600 Olympian feet, 190 metres) long. That's why we have sports 'stadiums' today. The competitors raced up and down, not round and round.

10 The poet Homer described a race between Odysseus and Achilles. Odysseus was losing and said a quick prayer to the goddess, Athene. She not only made Achilles slip – she made him fall head first into cattle droppings. He stood up spitting cow dung – and lost the race, of course.

Funny food

Sacrificial snacks

A sacrifice is *supposed* to be a groovy gift to the gods. 'Here
you are, gods, here's a present for you. I'm being nice to you,
so you will be nice to me, won't you?'

When the Greeks sacrificed an animal to a god, they
roasted it and they ate it. That's a bit like buying your mum
a box of chocolates then scoffing them yourself.

- The greatest honour was to have some roasted heart,
  lungs, liver or kidney from the sacrificed animal.
- The best meat was shared around.
- Everything left was minced together and put into
  sausages or puddings – but the important people didn't
  bother with those.
- This didn't leave very much for the gods to eat, you
  understand. Just the tail, the thigh bones and the
  gall bladder.

The Greeks even mixed the blood and the fat together and
stuffed it into the bladder of the animal. They then roasted
and ate this little treat. Would you like to try this to see what
the Greeks ate? (Without all the mess of sacrificing a cow,
of course. That can make a terrible mess on the living-room
carpet.) Then go to your local butcher's shop and ask for it.
But what do you ask for?

1 haggis

2 black pudding

3 sausage

DON'T YOU THINK
YOU'RE TAKING THE
SACRIFICE THING
A LITTLE TOO FAR?

Did you know…?
Vegetarians in ancient Greece wouldn't sacrifice animals to the gods. Instead they sacrificed *vegetables* – groovy, eh?

Munching Milon

Milon was a wrestler. He also thought he was pretty groovy. Before one Olympic contest he walked around the stadium with a live young bull on his shoulders.

He fancied a snack after all that effort, so he killed the bull and ate it. He finished the whole bull before the day was out.

But maybe there are some gods on Olympus with a sense of fair play. Because, in the end, Milon got what he deserved. *Exactly* what he deserved.

It started with him showing off again. He split open a tree with his bare hands … but his hand became stuck in the split. Try as he might he couldn't get free. When a pack of wolves came along they licked their chops and moved in on Milon.

What did they do to Milon? Just what Milon did to the young bull – except they probably didn't cook him first.

Foul food

The Greeks ate the meat of sacrifices but didn't eat a lot of meat in their normal day-to-day lives. One historian

said, 'The Greeks had meals of two courses; the first a kind of porridge – and the second a kind of porridge.'

In fact it wasn't quite that bad. The 'porridge' was more a sort of paste made up of lentils, beans and com all ground up with oil – vegetable oil, not the sort of oil garages put in cars.

The peasants had some olives, figs, nuts or goats-milk cheese to add a bit of taste. They washed it down with water or goat's milk.

After about 500 BC the rich started to eat more meat than the peasants – goat, mutton, pork or deer - and drink wine rather than water. But what else did they eat of the following?

Spartan soup

You might not have enjoyed living in Athens and eating grasshoppers and thrushes. But you could have been worse off. You could have lived in Sparta.

The Spartans had a disgusting concoction called Black Broth. They mixed pork juices with salt and *vinegar* into a sort of soup.

The Athenians made some very cruel comments about Spartan food. Athenaeus said, 'The Spartans claim to be the bravest people in the world. To eat food like that they'd *have* to be.'

Another Athenian said, 'It isn't surprising the Spartans are ready to die on the battlefield – death has to be better than living on food like theirs.'

The groovy Greek guzzler

Archestratus wrote the first ever cookery book in Europe. It was written in verse and probably meant to be recited at feasts – not used as a recipe book. It contained some quirky bits of advice to eaters and to cooks. Archestratus seemed a rather grumpy man with strong views on some foods...

A Pontic fish, the Saperde,
Is poor and tasteless and it smells.
To those who eat this thing I say,
Both you and it can go to hell!

66

And Archestratus had his own favourite foods. He liked to rubbish more popular dishes…

Now some men like the taste of beef,
They sing the praises of the cow.
While I would rather get my teeth,
Into the belly of a sow.

But Archestratus saved his nastiest comments for foreign cooks who ruined good Greek food with their recipes...

If your food you want to waste,
Take a Bass fish from the sea,
Find a cook with awful taste
Like the cooks from Italy.

Syracuse has bad cooks too
Spoiling Bass in sauce of cheese,
Or in pickles, taste like glue,
Keep away from cooks like these.

Just as well he didn't live to taste our modern versions of Italian delights. He might have written a horrible verse like …

Spaghetti hoops that come in tins
Belong in deep and dusty bins.
As for tasteless plastic pizza
Simply leave it in your frizza.

Groovy Greek growing-up

Bother for babies

From 500 – 200 BC there was a ritual way of treating babies. Would *you* survive?

Father inspects baby. Is it fit?
Yes Go to **1**.
No Go to **2**.
Don't know Go to **5**.

1 If you have too many boys then they'll have to split up your land when you die. Too many girls will cost you money. Do you want to keep it?
Yes Go to **6**.
No Go to **2**.

2 Put the baby in a pot (a pithos), then leave baby on a hillside to die. Do you care?
Yes Go to **4**.
No Go to **3**.

3 Baby dies before it's a week old.

4 Let a childless couple know what's going on. They will get to it before the cold or the wolves do. Baby lives with foster parents.
Go to **6**.

5 Father will 'test' the baby by rubbing it with icy water, wine or urine (yeuch). Does it survive?
Yes Go to **6**.
No Go to **3**.

6 The baby is one of the family. Tell the world with an olive branch on the door if it's a boy, a piece of wool for a girl.
Go to **7**.

7 Hold the *Amphidromia* ceremony. When baby is seven days old, sweep the house and sprinkle it with water. Father holds baby and runs round hearth with it while family sings hymns.
Go to **8**.

8 When baby is ten days old have the naming ceremony. (A boy is named after his grandfather.) Congratulations – you've made it… unless disease or plague or war or something else gets you!

The good news: Boys didn't go to school until they were seven – girls didn't have to go to school at all.

The bad news: You didn't add up with numbers. You added up with letters – a = 1, b = 2, c = 3 and so on.

MUM'S GIVEN ME A 2-9-7 6-9-7 FOR DINNER! WONDER WHAT 4-1-4 8-1-4 ?

But do *you* know what number BAD + HEAD make?

Answer: 214 + 8514 = 8728

WHAT DOES *BAD* AND *HEAD* MAKE ?

A CASE FOR THE DOCTOR SIR!

The really bad news: Boys took a slave to school with them. No, *not* to do their work. The job of the slave was to make sure the boy behaved himself. If he didn't then the slave would give him a good beating.

Test your teacher

The Greeks loved thinking about things – the science of thinking about things became known as 'philosophy'. But it was a thinker from Italy who came up with the most curious thoughts – Zeno of Elea. The Greeks loved talking and thinking about Zeno's 'problems'. Test your teacher with this sneaky (and Greeky) question...

PLEASE, SIR, IMAGINE A RACE BETWEEN THE GREEK HERO, ACHILLES, AND A TORTOISE. ACHILLES RUNS TEN TIMES FASTER THAN THE TORTOISE: THE TORTOISE IS GIVEN A START OF TEN METRES. WILL ACHILLES EVER PASS THE TORTOISE?

HO HO HO. OF COURSE HE WILL!

WRONG! CLEVER MR ZENO OF ELEA SAID NO. EVERY TIME ACHILLES REACHES THE PLACE THE TORTOISE WAS, THE TORTOISE HAS MOVED FORWARD A TENTH OF THE DISTANCE THAT ACHILLES HAS RUN SO THE TORTOISE WILL ALWAYS BE AHEAD

ERR... UM

Surviving school dinners

Have you ever been to school dinners and seen nothing you fancy? What happens? You go hungry.

The Lydians went hungry for a very long time because there was a famine. They decided to do something about the problem. They discovered that the more you think about food the hungrier you get. So they invented games to take their minds off food. They played dice and knucklebones.

The games were so interesting they didn't notice they were hungry. The next day they ate whatever they could find but didn't play games. This went on for 18 years! Games one day, food the next.

So, if you don't fancy a school dinner then play knucklebones. You need five ankle-joints from *cloven-footed* animals. (They make neat cubes of bone.) There are several cloven-footed animals – bison, pigs, goats, antelopes and sheep. If any of those appear on a schooldinner menu then you might just be in luck.

If your school cook slaughters her own wildebeest in the kitchens, then ask her for the little cube-shaped bones from the ankle joint. If she *doesn't* then you'll just have to use small cubes of wood like dice.

Knucklebones: 'Horse in the Stable'

Players: One or more players.

You need: Five knucklebones (or wooden cubes).

Rules: Put four knucklebones on the ground. Each one is a 'horse'.

Put the left hand near them with the fingers and thumb tips spread out and touching the ground. The gaps between the fingers are the 'stables'.

One knucklebone is tossed into the air with the right hand.

Before catching it the player must knock one 'horse' into a 'stable' with the right hand – that is, they must flick a knucklebone into a gap between the fingers.

With the right hand, catch the knucklebone that was thrown in the air.

Repeat until all four 'horses' are in their 'stables' – no more than one 'horse' to a 'stable'!

If all four are put in their 'stables' then move the left hand away from the 'horses'. Toss the throwing stone into the air with the right hand, pick up all four horses with the right hand, and catch the throwing stone in the right hand.

If the turn ends with a full 'stable', or if the player makes a mistake, pass the turn to the next person.

The first to 'stable' all the 'horses' ten times is the winner!

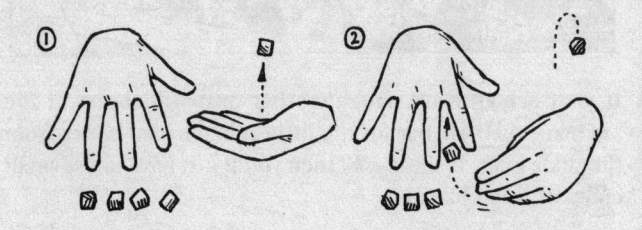

72

The school Olympics

Greek children invented games like knucklebones that are still played in some parts of the world today. In fact you may even have played some of the games yourself. If you haven't, and want to play like a groovy Greek, then here are the rules for six games.

Ostrakinda

This is a game for two teams that is still played in Italy, Germany and France. You need: A silver coin. Paint one side black with poster paint – this side is 'Night'. The plain side is 'Day'.

Rules: 1 Divide into two teams – the 'Nights' and the 'Days'.
2 Spin the coin in the air.
3 If it lands black side up then the Nights chase the Days – and if it lands silver side up the Days chase the Nights.

Cooking pot

Rules: 1 Choose someone to be 'It'.
2 'It' is blindfolded and sits on the ground.
3 The others try to touch or poke 'It'.
4 'It' aims to touch one of the teasers with a foot.
5 Anyone touched by a foot becomes 'It', is blindfolded and sat on the ground.

Bronze Fly

A sort of Greek Blind-man's Buff. A Greek described it...

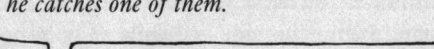

> They fastened a head-band round a boy's eyes.
> He was then turned round and round and called out, 'I will chase the bronze fly!'
> The others called back, 'You might chase him but you won't catch him.'
> They then torment him with paper whips until he catches one of them.

ISN'T THAT A BULL WHIP?

Ephedrismos

Rules:
1 A player is blindfolded and gives a second one a piggy-back.

2 The rider then has to guide the player to a target set on the ground.

3 If the player succeeds then he becomes the rider. This could become a competition where pairs race to reach the target.

ARE YOU SURE THIS IS THE WAY TO THE TARGET?

Greecket

The Greeks also played ball games where you throw a ball at a 'wicket', rather like cricket without a batsman.

We just have pictures of these games that have been painted on Greek vases, but we don't have their written rules. Make up your own rules – maybe they played like this...

1 Stand on a mark a fixed distance from the wicket.

2 Take the ball and have ten attempts to hit the wicket.

3 The opponent stands behind the wicket (like a wicket-keeper) and throws the ball back to you every time.

4 Then you stand behind the wicket while your opponent has ten tries.

5 The one who has the most hits of the wicket from ten throws is the winner.

6 Try again from a different mark.

It looks (from the vase paintings) as if the loser has to give the winner a piggy-back ride.

Kottabos

Rules: 1 Take a wooden pole and stand it upright.

2 Balance a small metal disk on top of the pole.

3 Leave a little wine in the bottom of your two-handled drinking cup.

4 Grip the cup by one handle, flick the wine out and try to knock the disk off the top of the pole.

NOT VERY GOOD ARE YOU?

(Would you believe grown-up Greeks played this silly game at parties?)

You can try this with a cup and water and a 50p coin on the end of a broom handle ... but not in your dining-room, please.

Puzzle your parents

So your parents think they're smart, do they? Give them this simple test to check their brain-power. All they have to do is answer 'Groovy Greeks', 'Terrible Tudors' or 'Vile Victorians'...

Who had these toys or games first? The Greeks, the Tudors or the Victorians?

1 puppets moved by strings

2 draughts

3 tug of war

4 dolls with moving parts

5 model chariots
6 yo–yos
7 babies' rattles
8 spinning-tops
9 see-saws
10 bowling hoops

Epilogue

After the groovy Greeks came the rotten Romans. The Romans were supposed to be an even greater people than the Greeks. After all, they eventually ruled over half the world – including Britain.

But the Romans were pretty rotten compared to the Greeks. Their games weren't great sports events like the Olympics – they were just an excuse to watch humans kill animals, animals kill humans, animals kill animals and humans kill humans. In boxing, for example, the Greeks bound their hands with leather bands like boxing gloves. The Romans bound their hands with leather bands – but put vicious spikes in them.

One story about the take-over of Greece by the Romans gives a good example of what the world lost when the rotten Romans took over from the groovy Greeks...

Archimedes was a brilliantly clever Greek. When the Romans attacked his people in the city of Syracuse (211 BC) Archimedes used his great and groovy brain to invent wonderful new weapons.

For two years the Romans were kept out of the city as the inventor created 'death-rays' – giant mirrors that reflected the sun on to Roman ships in the harbour and set them on fire – and huge catapults that drove them off.

But at last the Romans broke through the Greek defences and brought terror to the citizens of Syracuse as they killed and stole from the houses. The Roman commander had given one strict order, however: 'Find Archimedes – but

don't hurt the great man.'

At last a Roman soldier burst into Archimedes' house. The inventor was in the middle of an experiment and was too busy to bother with a small matter like an invasion at that moment.

The Roman was puzzled. Why was this old man ignoring him?

The Roman became angry. How *dare* this old man ignore him?

The Roman lost his cool. He killed the defenceless inventor. With one blow he destroyed one of the cleverest men the world has known.

The Roman soldier was punished for disobeying the commander's order not to harm Archimedes. But that didn't bring the old man back. Just as none of even the greatest Roman achievements could bring back the glory of the Greeks.

The rotten Romans ruled – the groovy Greeks went to their graves. That's horrible history for you.

It all started with a Scarecrow

Puffin is well over sixty years old.
Sounds ancient, doesn't it? But Puffin has never been
so lively. We're always on the lookout for the next big
idea, which is how it began all those years ago.

Penguin Books was a big idea from the mind of
a man called Allen Lane, who in 1935 invented
the quality paperback and changed the world.
**And from great Penguins, great Puffins grew,
changing the face of children's books forever.**

The first four Puffin Picture Books were hatched in 1940 and the
first Puffin story book featured a man with broomstick arms called
Worzel Gummidge. In 1967 Kaye Webb, Puffin Editor, started the
Puffin Club, promising to **'make children into readers'**.
She kept that promise and over 200,000 children became
devoted Puffineers through their quarterly installments of
Puffin Post, which is now back for a new generation.

Many years from now, we hope you'll look back and
remember Puffin with a smile. **No matter what your age
or what you're into, there's a Puffin for everyone.**
The possibilities are endless, but one thing is for sure:
whether it's a picture book or a paperback, a sticker book
or a hardback, **if it's got that little Puffin
on it – it's bound to be good.**

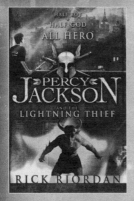